3

HUMAN RIGHTS
AND INTERNATIONAL ACTION

HUMAN RIGHTS
AND INTERNATIONAL ACTION

THE CASE OF FREEDOM OF ASSOCIATION

ERNST B. HAAS

STANFORD UNIVERSITY PRESS
STANFORD, CALIFORNIA
1970

Stanford University Press
Stanford, California
© 1970 by the Board of Trustees of the
Leland Stanford Junior University
Printed in the United States of America
ISBN 0-8047-0725-1
LC 77-107648

To David Mitrany
with respect and admiration

Preface

This study is an outgrowth of a long personal interest in the relationship between the functional theory of international integration and the organizational task of protecting human rights through international procedures and sanctions. Man, it is often said, cannot enjoy his inalienable rights because his own government violates them and no global agency exists to restrain the sovereign state. The obvious remedy is the creation of United Nations organs with power to persuade or compel national governments to respect the rights of their citizens. Functionalism, both as a strategy of political action and as a method of scholarly analysis, has a particular interest in the question of human rights. As a strategy of political action, the functional approach wishes to create intimate ties between man the individual and international agencies in order to reduce the role of the national government as the sole font of authority and loyalty; functional analysis singles out processes and attitudes that tend to detract from the dominance of the nation-state as a means of charting the evolution—if any—of a tighter and larger web of international interdependence.

The fact remains, however, that the functional approach to the study of human rights is strictly a second-best approach. Functionalism is marked by a reliance on incremental processes of change, on indirection, on the instrumental but temporary character of actor motives; the demand for human rights by sweeping claims, quasi-religious fervor, impatience with negotiation and compromise, intimations of the coming millennium. Why dim the flame of hope with the chill calculation of costs and benefits, long-term gains and short-term losses?

The answer ought to be clear: the direct, passionate, and consummatory approach to the question of protecting human rights by international means has failed! There appears to be very little in the way of genuine freedom, either for the individual or for groups (other than nations, real or claimed), that has been achieved through the constantly growing number of UN declarations and conventions dealing with human rights. International rhetoric is certainly flourishing. But whether rhetoric results in law, and law in new attitudes and increased rights at the national level, is not at all clear. The legal definition of human rights, as contained in comprehensive documents such as the International Covenant on Civil and Political Rights, has yet to demonstrate its prowess as a changer of attitudes and policies, since the machinery for translating legal phrases into national policy has not been tested.

Functionalism, though second-best, is still a useful approach because it can help us contrive a test. If the direct and global approach to protect man against his own government has brought little in the way of results, it remains possible, at least, that the indirect and modest functional approach can bring less spectacular but more solid results. This thought contains a theoretical as well as an empirical kernel. On the theoretical front, functionalism could provide an approach toward the more effective protection of human rights because it takes for granted—even capitalizes on—certain Hobbesian aspects of international life; it could provide a theory for turning vice into a servant of eventual virtue. This study presents a paradigm for envisaging and testing such a possibility. Empirically, functionalism provides the analytical tools for discovering whether current practices in certain international organizations tend to support the theory of progress by guile and indirection. The materials for the test are available. They are used in this study, suggested by the theory of functionalism.

In short, this study argues that unless the protection of human rights is approached in the functional context, nothing much can be expected from the UN or international law. But it also suggests that even the functional approach, as a strategy of political action, may well turn out to be inadequate to protect man against his own government. Functionalism, as a method of analysis, is used to test this suspicion. Unfortunately for man, even the second-best hope does not pass the test.

Work on this theme was initiated in the context of my *Beyond the Nation-State*, though my focus there was on the evolution of an organizational task in contrast to my present concern with the transformation of values at the national level. The test of the functional logic is provided by the only aspect of international human rights protection machinery sufficiently developed to provide adequate materials: the International Labor Organization's machinery for protecting freedom of association. Freedom of association is thus used as an elaborate case study to examine the utility of the functional strategy. I have recoded and reanalyzed the materials presented in the earlier work; I have added an analysis of all cases brought before the ILO between 1963 and 1968; and I have brought the analysis into overall focus by examining the impact of the machinery on the evolution of a world consensus on human rights. Since the year 1968, International Human Rights Year, gave rise to a large number of studies and analyses of this subject, I have been able to include and profit from this additional work.

This study is part of a larger project of the Institute of International Studies, University of California (Berkeley), entitled "Studies in International Integration." I take this opportunity to express my gratitude for financial and other support, both to the Institute and to the Ford Foundation. I am grateful also to Michael Rubner and Elizabeth Schorske for devoted, painstaking, and exemplary research assistance, which approached real collaboration. Harvey Weinstein arranged for computer programming services. The study profited from the comments of Professors David Mitrany, Harold Jacobson, Jean Siotis, and Ehud Harari, and from discussion with various officials of the ILO. It also owes much to the scrutiny of Dr. Richard Scott, formerly legal advisor to the United Nations Educational, Scientific and Cultural Organization and currently on the staff of the Organization for Economic Cooperation and Development. Peter Haas helped with computations, and Kathleen Wilson typed the manuscript and prepared the index. I am especially grateful to Professor Edward T. Rowe for permitting the use of unpublished data. Responsibility for errors of fact and interpretation remains mine alone.

E.B.H.

Berkeley, California
Summer 1969

Contents

List of Tables

Abbreviations

ECOSOC	United Nations Economic and Social Council
GATT	General Agreement on Tariffs and Trade
GGCL	Greek General Confederation of Labor
ICFTU	International Confederation of Free Trade Unions
ICJ	International Court of Justice
IFCTU	International Federation of Christian Trade Unions (World Democratic Labor Movement)
ILO	International Labor Organization
OAS	Organization of American States
UN	United Nations
UNCTAD	United Nations Conference on Trade and Development
UNESCO	United Nations Educational, Scientific, and Cultural Organization
UNITAR	United Nations Institute for Training and Research
WFTU	World Federation of Trade Unions

HUMAN RIGHTS
AND INTERNATIONAL ACTION

1. *Introduction*

In the spring of 1968, a year heralded as International Human Rights Year by the UN General Assembly, the world's governments proclaimed certain principles to be universal. At the International Conference on Human Rights that met at Teheran in April and May, they declared:

> It is imperative that the members of the international community fulfill their solemn obligations to promote and encourage respect for human rights and fundamental freedoms for all without distinctions of any kind such as race, color, sex, language, religion, political or other opinions.
>
> The Universal Declaration of Human Rights states a common understanding of the peoples of the world concerning the inalienable and inviolable rights of all members of the human family and constitutes an obligation for the members of the international community.
>
> Gross denials of human rights arising from discrimination on grounds of race, religion, belief or expression of opinion outrage the conscience of mankind and endanger the foundations of freedom, justice and peace in the world.[1]

On the same occasion, the same governments found that all human rights conventions and declarations "have created new standards and obligations to which states should conform"; that each individual is entitled to maximum freedom and dignity; that *apartheid*, racism, and colonialism constitute crimes against humanity; that the realization of human rights on a global scale demands massive development policies so that economic, social, and cultural rights can be enjoyed by all; that illiteracy is a denial of human rights, as is the subordination of women and children; and that all peoples have a right to family planning. Finally, said the delegates, savings realized from world disarmament must be invested in the promotion of human rights.*

Are we to take these stirring words as an expression of a new global consensus on the inalienable rights of the individual? The conference urged the UN Commission on Human Rights to prepare a model procedural code to guide other UN bodies that have, or may acquire, the power to implement rather than merely invoke human rights. But the conference made no specific suggestions for the creation of UN supervisory organs, conciliation commissions, ombudsmen, or investigative agencies.[2] This oversight suggests that the reiteration of stirring words should not be accepted as evidence for the arrival of a new dawn of global freedom.

UNIVERSAL VALUE CONSENSUS OR COMPETITIVE COEXISTENCE?

The absence of any marked concern with machinery to enforce these rights is not the only reason one tends to doubt that a verbal concern with human rights and freedoms is evidence of impressive progress toward a global community with shared values. It is sometimes said that generous words reflect the normative dimension of politics, and the cynical action or inaction of governments the em-

---

* The proclamation was adopted unanimously by the 84 states that sent delegations. In addition, the conference adopted 28 other resolutions, many on bitterly divided votes. Ten further proposals were not acted on but were forwarded to the UN for consideration. The most strongly contested resolutions included the customary condemnations of colonialism, racial discrimination, South Africa, Rhodesia, Portugal, Great Britain, and NATO. Others that were well debated were in the form of demands: for the economic redistribution program of the UN Conference on Trade and Development; for disarmament, family planning, legal aid, literacy campaigns, and improvement of education; for guarantees of the rights of children, refugees, and prisoners of war; and for protection against the threat to the human personality implicit in the evolution of science and technology. With the exception of the novel and vitally important concern about science and technology, these demands had all been made before on many occasions in various UN bodies.

pirical. But this distinction will not help us resolve the present paradox: when 84 governments invoke generous words, draft conventions, vote for them, and occasionally even ratify them, the empirical dimension is in fact at work; but subsequent inaction is just as empirical. The true conundrum between empirical words and empirical deeds is more complex.

One way to conceptualize the paradox is to juxtapose the universal invocation of human rights in the UN to the regional pattern of activity. If the growth of UN conventions, covenants, declarations, and commissions is to be interpreted as a march toward a value consensus, it must then be contrasted with the even more pronounced march in this area on the part of European, Latin American, and African regional efforts. But far from mutually reinforcing each other, these trends may be in competition, possibly stressing different rights, different values, and different procedures. The divided votes at Teheran expressed quite clearly the tension between a façade of universalism and the reality of competing regionalisms. One may well ask, then, who is being integrated with whom and at whose expense, when the trend toward a universal articulation of common values must compete with simultaneous but clashing regional efforts?

One may consider also the definition of universal norms and values, as well as the desire to cement a universal status quo or at least fix a minimum common denominator among all values. Votes, such as the unanimous ones at Teheran, define the empirical outline of the common denominator for the time. But again, the divided votes illustrate the presence of regionally shared values within the universal ones, values that pit one region against another. Which values will prevail? The future of the UN as a catalyst of value sharing is in the balance, for the character of the eventual synthesis will determine whether we shall have greater universal value consensus or merely value conflict among regions, mediated from the center.[3]

Hence there is little comfort in Frederick van Asbeck's injunction—true though it may be—that the real purpose in studying international law is "to explore how the present law has come to be what it is, how it is involved in a process of reform and extension and intensification, in order that we may be able to assist in the building, stone upon stone, in storm and rain, of a transnational legal order for states and peoples and men."[4] Nor does it help much to know that we ought to work for a public and civic order for all mankind, and particularly to adopt "human dignity as the postulated aim of jurisprudence, understanding this to embrace within the world commonwealth all men everywhere, and to imply a universe of wide rather than narrow participation in the shaping and sharing of values."[5] This legal order, and even the indirect and functional process of approaching it, would undoubtedly be ushered in through a convincing program of defining and enforcing internationally determined human rights. But how can it, unless we determine when and whether the UN is creating a new global value consensus?

We can approach an answer if we study systematically the UN experience with the active protection of human rights, instead of contenting ourselves with reciting the texts of conventions and declarations and submitting them to legal exegesis. To do so, moreover, is to grant that *if* human rights activity tends to take place at a level higher than the minimum rhetorical denominator among states and regions, the global sharing and integration of values is indeed going forward. In short, the study of human rights in the UN is an interesting diagnostic device to discover whether the world is shrinking or not.

Human rights are particularly appropriate in this connection because they involve, by definition, international norms and values. The process of negotiating and defining them—particularly if it requires almost 20 years, as in the case of the International Covenant on Civil and Political Rights and the Covenant on Economic, Social and Cultural Rights—could be considered a socializing experience for the participants. The reiteration and invocation of these norms so defined in international and national texts could be expected to confirm the socialization further. Even if we grant that the substructure of national values that went into the definition of the international norms is rich in its variety and contrast, the enforcement and implementation of new internationally sanctioned norms must gradually influence and even transform the national ones. Implementation will tend to make values more and more globally homogeneous; concurrently, national institutions and attitudes will approximate one another globally. "Stone upon stone, in storm and rain," as Van Asbeck said, a global community of shared values and institutions could be ushered in as the UN works first against genocide, then against slavery and racial discrimination, and finally against all forms of religious intolerance—not to mention the shotgun approach on all fronts epitomized by the two covenants.

UNIVERSAL VALUE SHARING AND ENFORCEMENT OF NORMS

One might suppose that the trend toward uniformity and value sharing would be enhanced if UN machinery to supervise the protection of human rights were to be established. Even though the Teheran Conference did not stress this feature, two such mechanisms have already been established and a third is close to being adopted by the UN. Similar procedures are used by the ILO and UNESCO. Table 1 summarizes the various provisions for supervising the enforcement of norms, including the important obligation of submitting regular reports for review by a supervisory organ. Five conventions call for special committees to supervise implementation and receive complaints, the only such agencies functioning or projected in the UN system at the moment. It is possible, then, that the infrastructure for promoting uniformity of values by way of central supervision is being built under our eyes. Each of the five committees may become the font of an authoritative jurisprudence on human rights.

The completion of the two international covenants on human rights is merely the most spectacular innovation in the field of fostering global values. The very full catalogue of substantive rights is marked by an absence of complaint machinery in the case of the Covenant on Economic, Social and Cultural Rights; the Covenant on Civil and Political Rights, though equally comprehen-

TABLE 1

Supervisory and Enforcement Provisions in Human Rights Conventions

Provision	Genocide[a]	International labor code[b]	ILO: freedom of association[c]	Discrimination in education[d]	Civil and political rights[e]	Racial discrimination[f]	Religious intolerance[g]
Entry into force	1951	1919	1950	1962–68	—	1969	—
Must states report regularly on implementation?	no	yes; to a permanent body of experts	only to committee of experts	yes; to UNESCO Gen. Confer.	yes; to committee	yes; to committee	yes; to ECOSOC
May state members lodge complaints?	yes; to UN organs	yes; to ILO organs	no	yes; to committee	yes; to committee	yes; to committee	yes; to committee
May nongovernmental organizations lodge complaints?	no	yes	yes	no	no	yes; under special protocol	yes; under special declaration
May individuals lodge complaints?	no	no	no	no	yes; under special protocol	yes; under special protocol	yes; under special declaration
Is there a standing committee to hear complaints?	no	no	yes	yes	yes	yes	yes
Is the committee's jurisdiction compulsory?	—	—	yes	yes	no; needs special declaration	yes (except for individual petitions)	yes (except for individual petitions)
Is the committee composed of experts acting in personal capacity?	—	—	no	yes	yes	yes	yes

	a	b	c	d	e	f	g
Is the committee to seek a friendly settlement?	—	—	yes	yes	yes	yes	yes
Can committee create ad hoc conciliation commission?	—	ILO organs may	yes	yes	no	yes	no
Is conciliation commission's jurisdiction compulsory?	—	yes	no	—	no	no	—
Can committee publish adverse report as most severe sanction?	—	yes	yes	yes	no; simply publish facts	yes	yes
Provision for appeal to International Court of Justice?	yes	yes	no	yes	no	yes	yes

a Convention on the Prevention and Punishment of the Crime of Genocide, UN *Treaty Series*, Vol. 78, p. 277. Articles 8, 9. Parties in 1969: 73.

b ILO, *Constitution* (as amended May 20, 1954), Articles 19, 22, 24–29, 31, 32.

c This procedure developed ad hoc in the Governing Body, following adoption of an authorizing resolution by ECOSOC. *Fourth Report of the International Labour Organisation to the United Nations* (Geneva, 1950), pp. 322–28.

d UNESCO, *Protocol Instituting a Conciliation and Good Offices Committee to be Responsible for Seeking a Settlement of any Disputes which May Arise between States Parties to the Convention Against Discrimination in Education*, Articles 2, 11, 14, 15, 21. Parties to convention: 50; to protocol: 18. (May 30, 1969.)

e International Covenant on Civil and Political Rights, *UN Monthly Chronicle* (February 1967), Articles 28, 40–42; optional protocol to the International Covenant on Civil and Political Rights, Articles 1, 4, 5. Not in force. One ratification for covenant and protocol, as of Jan. 1, 1969.

f International Convention on the Elimination of Racial Discrimination, *UN Monthly Chronicle* (January 1966), Articles 8, 9, 11–14, 21. Parties: 27 (Jan. 1, 1969).

g Draft articles submitted to the Commission on Human Rights by the Sub-Commission on Prevention of Discrimination and Protection of Minorities for inclusion in the Draft International Convention on the Elimination of All Forms of Religious Intolerance. Commission on Human Rights, *Report on 23rd Session* (20 February–23 March 1967), UN doc. E/4322, E/CN.4/940, pp. 36–40. No action was taken on this proposal during 1968.

sive substantively, possesses a weak supervisory and enforcement mechanism. The UNESCO Conciliation and Good Offices Commission, which oversees the execution of the convention against discrimination in education, lacks jurisdiction over individual complaints and therefore tends to pit state against state.[6] Only the two texts seeking to eliminate racial discrimination and religious intolerance combine a series of specifically defined rights with anything approaching a complete supervisory and enforcement system.

Much legal opinion supports the proposition that the sum of these activities represents a quantitative breakthrough in favor of a new shared concern with freedom. Many lawyers see the Universal Declaration of Human Rights as occupying a middle position between binding obligation and simple declaration—not law but "laws in the making because invocation in national and international texts has given them legitimacy."[7] They find direct evidence of such invocation in the constitutions of ten new countries, in the 19 other constitutions that reflect the declaration's principles, and in the six national legislative enactments that refer to the declaration.[8] Other lawyers assert that there is a powerful link between the protection of human rights and the preservation of peace. Rosalyn Higgins contends that the General Assembly has jurisdiction over situations involving a breach of certain Charter provisions dealing with human rights because Articles 55 and 56 are specifically binding norms, not merely declaratory in character, an argument first advanced by Hersch Lauterpacht.[9] Hence resolutions designed to enforce human rights provisions do not infringe the Charter prohibition against intervention. And this would hold true regardless of whether such violations arise in conjunction with a potential or an imminent threat to peace, provided that an impartial investigation of the facts is made first.

But the cynic may still ask whether all this activity and argumentation presages a true commitment to universal norms and procedures, or whether it merely amounts to a use of the rhetoric of human rights in the service of national policy, regional self-assertion, or international propaganda. The legislative history of the conventions, and especially of their provisions for enforcement, suggests a wide divergence of national expectations regarding the utility and feasibility of uniform development.[10] Some lawyers tend to think the current effort represents so much ritual posturing, unless several other steps are taken. The practical obstacles to effective implementation must be faced and the causes of violations determined. "Much—much more—must be learned about what causes widespread denials of human rights and how these causes can be attacked. Moreover, such denials must be treated as what they are—as complex social problems whose solution requires a variety of social tools rather than as Sunday school exercises in good and evil."[11] Specifically, more stress must be placed on technical assistance, advisory services, and local programs rather than global declarations, on dispassionate fact-finding to free human rights issues from the political propaganda context in which they are often embedded. Spectacular rewards for compliance must be offered. More attention should be paid to regional human rights procedures. Most importantly for our purposes, piecemeal agreements should be sought, isolating specific rights for intensive treatment. It is in the context of the piecemeal and incremental approach to the protection of human rights that the experience of the ILO is preferred by the few who are familiar with it to the more spectacular comprehensive approach of the UN.

INCREMENTALISM, VALUE CHANGE, AND THE DIVERSITY OF REGIMES

Neither the human rights enthusiast nor the cynical commentator has settled the controversy. Both have hold of part of the truth, but their arguments tend to obscure the path by which countries and their peoples may come to approximate each other's values and institutions. This path accepts that countries may demand action in the field of human rights for self-seeking purposes—that the rhetoric of the debate may be more important to them than enforcement, and a burst of righteous anger more important than a calculated and long-range effort. The point is, if *certain kinds* of human rights are singled out for common action, whatever the momentary motives for government action, they do not determine the outcome of that action insofar as an eventual growth of a value consensus is concerned. Essentially, then, what we have elsewhere called the functional logic suggests how consensus can flow from conflict, unintended value confluence from intended confrontation. This logic holds, briefly, that some activities are too technical and specific to occasion controversy and thus lead to value consensus on so narrow a base as to be politically irrelevant; whereas broad and sweeping commitments papering over substantial conflict fail to result in a common task and value change—by the very fact of their controversial nature. Only the path of incremental steps—first attracting a specific clientele, later responding to growing demands by other constituencies, and finally transcending the particular coalition of selfish forces that began the program—has a real chance of fashioning a value consensus.[12] This much is true of any international action program; it is particularly true with respect to human rights because these are value-impregnated to a much greater extent, and are thus able to trigger consensus or conflict more rapidly and more passionately than programs dealing with telecommunications services, public health, nuclear radiation, or even arms control.

The resolutions of the Teheran Conference suggest that practically any kind of human concern is part of the struggle for human rights: decolonization, disarmament, economic development, even birth control! We cannot accept such a definition and still expect to say anything systematic about the incremental process of protecting human rights and developing a value consensus thereby. I agree that to cut the field down to size requires an emphasis on "defining agreed minimal standard 'inalienable rights' to which all human beings and collectivities can be viewed as entitled and by which the performance of governments can be measured."[13] These are the kinds of rights that are preeminently political and civil. The right to life and liberty, the right to vote, the right to free speech and assembly are not only valued on their own account; more important, perhaps, the substantive enjoyment of these rights is instrumental, vitally instrumental, for the achievement of other rights in the economic and social fields. The rights covered by the major international conventions tabulated in Table 1 should provide the core for a full-scale functional study, though we can present only data relating to freedom of association.

But even in the absence of systematic data, a functional approach to the study of human rights seems indicated: our daily newspapers tell us that the sweeping and direct attack on the protection of human rights by international means has not borne fruit. Despite the genocide convention, acts seemingly similar to genocide have occurred in Nigeria, Indonesia, Brazil, and Rwanda, without any serious effort being made to call the governments concerned to account under the provisions of the convention. Despite the civil libertarian tone of large parts of the International Covenant on Civil and Political Rights, divergent practices with respect to political freedom evidently have not declined; witness the immense increase in diversity of regimes and legal systems in the world over the last 20 years. Many argue that political repression and the persecution of dissent are more widely practiced than ever before. Certainly it cannot be argued that the divisions in the three "worlds" of today over major value commitments concerning individualism and personal choice have been diminished because of treaties dealing with statelessness, refugees, slavery, and the nationality of married women. It is possible that the Convention on the Political Rights of Women is at least associated with a growing world consensus in this realm, but whether religious toleration is on the increase because of greater tolerance or because of growing agnosticism may well be debated. Of all the many rights protected by the International Labor Code, only the protection against forced labor has enjoyed the benefit of international concern, supervision, and inquiry to any significant degree, a point to which we shall return.

Since governments embrace the international protection of human rights for selfish and expedient reasons, things could hardly be otherwise. Does that mean we are wasting our time in even examining the field of human rights for evidence of increasing value sharing among nations? Not necessarily. A functional approach to the study of human rights demands less of governments than does the formal, legal approach. It grants that consideration of immediate benefits is foremost in the minds of decision-makers; hence it is able to pinpoint governmental adaptations, and changes in perspective when an initial motive for action has run its course. Such an approach can open our eyes to the possible consequences of governmental initiatives, consequences that can have real importance for human rights and value sharing even though they were not intended by the decision-makers.

This perspective demands some appreciation of when and how the motives of governments and of private groups undergo change, as explained below. It also demands a recognition that a functional approach to the protection of human rights must proceed differently than the direct, global, legal, and comprehensive approach, as represented by the UN in the past. And even then functionalism may be no more effective as an agent of value change than the direct approach! Only the case-by-case evidence we have will suggest an answer.

But why opt for a strategy that is clearly second-best? Why focus on indirection and on the guile of history? The lack of success that has attended the direct approach is not sufficient justification. The fact is, a second-best strategy may be the best strategy when it, more successfully than any other, throws into focus one crucially important variable. In our case, that variable is the diversity of the nations and regimes that are supposed to be the beneficiaries of a global system of human rights. Diversity of power, ideology, culture, and objective is the key to understanding the real world. Unless ways are found to synthesize diverse perceptions and aspirations, it makes little sense even to consider the creation of universal norms and universal values. Our empirical material will stress diversity in political and economic institutions and objectives precisely in order to discover how much synthesizing has taken place *despite* increasing international heterogeneity.

The growing diversity of the world's polities is evident in the figures in Table 2. The categories will be defined in greater detail below. Note here only that the percentage of democratic regimes and of traditional oligarchies has declined consistently since 1950, and that mobilization regimes and authoritarian polities hostile to individual and group freedom have flourished, primarily in the

TABLE 2

Evolution of Types of Polities

(*per cent of total membership of the UN*)

Year	Number of UN members	Reconciliation polity	Mobilization polity	Traditional oligarchy	Modernizing oligarchy	Modernizing autocracy	Authoritarian polity
1946	53	43%	11%	34%	4%	6%	2%
1950	60	50	13	25	5	5	2
1953	61	46	13	19	8	7	7
1958	82	43	19	10	6	15	7
1967	120	37	18	5	5	10	25

Note: Ukraine and Byelorussia are not included.

economically underdeveloped regions of the world and in the wake of the decolonization movement. This diversity of regimes can be counteracted by international measures, providing that the governments of mobilization and authoritarian nations prove amenable to the texts and supervisory actions of the UN and its associated agencies. Whether in fact they do is a matter for empirical investigation.

One sharp distinction has to be made between new nations and old. As Dag Hammarskjöld put it: "It is natural for old and well-established countries to see in the United Nations a limitation on their sovereignty. It is just as natural that a young country, a country emerging on the world stage, should find in the United Nations an addition to its sovereignty, an added means of speaking to the world."[14] A system for protecting human rights might conceivably be acceptable to older nations ready, in principle, to give up the sovereignty fetish; but new nations join international organizations to strengthen their independence, not to water it down in favor of some superimposed system of norms! Are they therefore likely to abide by international norms established largely by others? Are they willing to submit their practices to the same scrutiny they wish to have focused on their erstwhile colonial masters? "No sane man wishes international busybodies to take over the responsibilities of local magistrates," says Jenks. "But, subject to appropriate safeguards against the abuse of international procedures, there is a real need for arrangements which ensure that the writ of human freedom runs everywhere. Only those who are prepared to accept service of that writ themselves have any moral claim to serve it upon others."[15] We are entitled to wonder whether new and old nations in fact have the same moral claim, in view of their different attitudes toward international organizations. But only an analysis that recognizes the diversity of regimes and their aims can provide the evidence to dispel (or confirm) our doubt.

The distinction between old and new nations leads to another aspect of diversity: the stress on the rights of the individual as opposed to the rights of collectivities. Human rights, as a concept of Western origin, has usually been associated with limiting the power of the state in order to assure the individual maximum freedom of action. Somewhat later this notion was expanded to include the collective rights of voluntary groups as against the state. In fact, the theory of the pluralist society and polity is predicated in large part on the ability of voluntary groups, free of legal restraint, to assert their claims against one another and against the state. Pluralism, and the free competition of ideas as well as of political influence, are firmly associated with one attitude toward human rights, most notably perceived in the protection of the right to freedom of association. Though the emphasis on restraining the state is by no means a monopoly of old nations, it tends to be found most commonly in democratic countries, which are, overwhelmingly, Western. Moreover, this emphasis bears a considerable relationship to the degree of economic and social development. Ample economic resources facilitate bargaining between groups; an expanding resource base makes possible a more relaxed attitude toward the unimposed division of the national product. In short, there is good reason to associate the emphasis on individual and group rights with democracy, industrialism, and capitalism.*

* Jenks proposes an attempt be made to universalize gradually certain principles of individual freedom well anchored in Western national and regional conventions and practices. He mentions the presumption of innocence, the avoidance of guilt by association, and the prohibition of retroactive penalties. International conventions establishing these three rights would be helpful in making the Covenant on Civil and Political Rights more effective than he considers it likely to be as it stands. See C. Wilfred Jenks, *Law in the World Community* (New York: David McKay, 1967), pp. 28–29.

Conversely, there are excellent grounds for a different attitude toward human rights to prevail in non-democratic and late-developing countries. There, collective rights are stressed, rights intended to strengthen state power to permit governmental modernization programs. Such rights may include national self-determination and the public ownership of natural resources. Another might be the right to be free from the "subversive" influence of "selfish" groups likely to interfere with the plans of the state. Socialist regimes with totalitarian institutions are far from accepting the notion of human rights in the same sense as the democracies. The situation is somewhat different in the case of other types of authoritarian regimes: they usually lack an ideological basis for denying the exercise of individual rights, but they effectively deny them just the same. Moreover, though less ready to create an ideological justification for stressing collective rights at the expense of the individual, in practice they frequently emphasize the state's power to plan, and therefore depart from the bias for individual rights that is common in traditional Western law.

In short, the widening gulf between a concept of human rights linked to individual freedom and a concept of human rights linked to collective strength is highly correlated with the type of regime in power and the degree of economic development that prevails. A paradigm that would suggest what kinds of rights are susceptible of international action and likely agents of universal value change simply cannot ignore the fact of world diversity. Indeed, such a paradigm must make heavy allowance for differences in political regime and economic development.

Another source of world diversity is equally important for our paradigm: the wide variation in economic institutions, prevailing or planned. Capitalist institutions nurtured the growth of individual rights; the group rights of trade unions and employers developed when capitalist industrialism finally recognized that labor was more than a commodity. Since that time, however, "mixed" economic institutions have been devised in the West, retaining many capitalist features but adding social security, monetary and fiscal policy, counter-cyclical calculation, and even indicative planning.

The fact is, we now have, in the practices and institutions we call the welfare state, implications of a great deal of centralization in economic institutions no longer under the control of individual entrepreneurs, large firms, or even an impersonal market. Meanwhile, socialist economic institutions have grown up in many parts of the world, with different claims on the citizen and a different vision of the welfare state. It has been suggested that the very success of the welfare state and its policies—overwhelmingly demanded in old and young nations alike—calls for powers of planning and control that are at variance with many traditional notions of individual human rights. Assuming a situation in which man has to choose between his right to social security benefits and his right to free speech, it would be hazardous to make a flat prediction that he would always opt for free speech. The more determined a regime to create economic institutions capable of realizing mass welfare, the more doubtful the possibility of protecting individual rights, nationally or internationally.[16]

This suggests that individual rights can no longer be meaningfully protected at all. But one corrective for this prediction is implicit in functional analysis and must therefore be made explicit in our paradigm. It may be possible to define new rights that protect individuals and voluntary groups against the welfare-maximizing state by singling out rights specific to a given policy area. It may also be possible to devise procedures for protecting those rights only, instead of attempting the ever more difficult problem of defining rights globally, irrespective of the policy area in which violations are likely to arise. Several possibilities come to mind: rights specific to workers in certain industries; the right of protection against an abuse of power by physicians or biologists; the right of peasants to be protected against certain land development measures, against forced labor, against excessive rural credit terms, all of which could become an issue in developing nations. In short, emphasis on a *given* policy area and a *given* group of people within it might still provide a way for limiting the power of the state, a power that most people ardently support on grounds of more effective welfare policies.

A final point: such a development would, in all likelihood, foster the evolution of voluntary, politically conscious groups. Moreover, those groups would probably have to exist, at least in embryonic form, before such rights could be made effective. Voluntary groups, in the logic of pluralism, provide both the initial constituency and the eventual lobby for anchoring and expanding human rights. Certainly it would be better if whole populations could demand and enjoy such rights, better for them and better for the eventual international sharing of important values. But if the various kinds of diversities we have sketched characterize the contemporary world system, then the piecemeal attack on human rights through specific constituencies and selected voluntary groups provides, not the second-best, but the *only* road to a different order.

On the other hand it is highly instructive to contrast these trends toward diversity with the voting records of the major regional clusters in the UN General Assembly. It would appear that governments entertain a somewhat schizophrenic attitude toward the international protection of human rights. Figures 1 and 2 plot the "human rights scores" of the major regions as revealed by the support or nonsupport of their member states for General Assembly resolutions relating to human rights. Fig. 1 shows scores based on all resolutions with such a content, including Cold War propaganda, efforts to shake colonial rule and policies, and attacks on *apartheid* in South Africa. Though far from united in 1946, most of the world's regions—except the West—have tended toward a score supporting strong human rights measures, clustering in the upper third of the scale. This is as true of Arab dictatorships, communist regimes, and African one-party states as it is of some Latin American and Asian democracies. As conduct at home showed less respect for human rights, international posturing showed more!

But once we control for the highly politicized issues, the picture changes somewhat. Fig. 2 is based on votes dealing with general human rights resolutions as well as such specific issues as the treatment of refugees, racial and religious discrimination, political rights, welfare issues, rights of women, and rights of the arrested. Now it is the Asian, communist, and Arab nations that show pro-

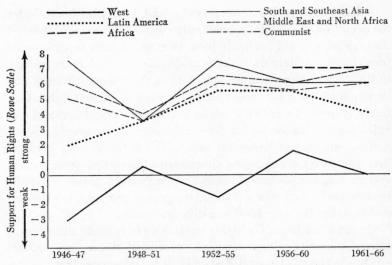

Fig. 1. *Human Rights Votes in UN General Assembly: All Issues*

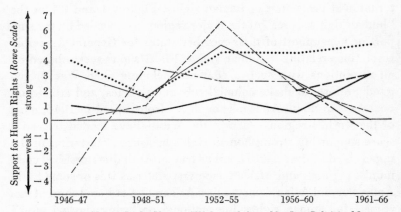

Fig. 2. *Human Rights Votes in UN General Assembly: Less Politicized Issues*

This material was made available to me through the courtesy of Edward T. Rowe. The Rowe Scale is computed as follows. All contested roll-call votes on all resolutions dealing in whole or in part with human rights, whether occurring in committee or in plenary session, were collected. Each resolution was examined to determine whether a vote for (or against) it could be considered "strong" or "weak" support for internationally protected human rights; if such a judgment was not possible the vote was excluded. Each state was then assigned a "human rights" score, which is the average, for each period, of the separate votes cast by that state coded according to whether it implied "strong" or "weak" support for human rights, as determined by the content of the resolution. Strongest possible support = 1.00 and weakest possible support = −1.00; in the figures above, the decimal point was moved one digit. All human rights votes: n = 585. Less politicized human rights votes: n = 205.

gressively less interest in internationally protected rights, as well as nationally practiced rights. The West shows a slight increase in support and Latin American support continues high. These scores express only trends in verbal support and say nothing about practice or true commitment; but they clearly show the lack of congruence between words and deeds and the uneven evolution of behavior among regions that provide the evidence for increasing world value diversity.

THE FUNCTIONAL LOGIC AND INTERNATIONAL CONVENTIONS

Why concentrate on political rights when we know that at any given time a sizable percentage of governments pay only lip service to them at home while loudly denouncing their opponents abroad for violations?[17] Because the character of a regime at one point in time is not the best and final indicator of the learning ability of a successor regime. Further, the history of certain human rights activities—notably protection against forced labor, slavery, and the persecution of trade unions—suggests that international norms can grow up *despite* the fact that the concern originated in a setting of conflict and vituperation among governments.[18] The advocacy of human rights commonly serves governments as an instrument for the assertion of different values: to end colonialism, to combat the alleged imperialism of international corporations, to stigmatize communism. Because such advocacy may play a part in advancing national self-determination, the evoking of inalienable human rights as an argument against colonialism may push a post-colonial government toward the observation of these norms at some later date. Even though the asserted direct link between world peace and human rights is largely spurious, a period of relative tranquility may favor the institutionalization of political rights as an unintended but real consequence after the initial period of propaganda is past. The advocacy of human rights—substantively and in terms of that advocacy opening a procedure for the enunciation of new rights—is "strategic" for international value sharing because it permits an outcome different from the initial intent of the advo-

cates. More formally, it is an issue capable of outliving the environment in which it was first raised.

If properly exploited, international norms lacking any real con-
sensual basis despite their enshrinement in conventions may aid in
feeding a pluralistic trend in member nations open to international
criticism. They can also encourage more rational and orderly procedures for resolving conflict nationally and internationally. If
enough regimes are transformed in the direction of what we shall
call "reconciliation polities," the character of the international organizations to which they belong would also be changed. Put differently, one unintended consequence of the international protection of human rights may be the socialization of new regimes into
an international rationality that stresses negotiation, fact-finding,
compromise, and moderation. If properly used, the norms and
mechanisms created for the international protection of human
rights could become a powerful device for bringing about a value
consensus. The point is that this consensus cannot be inferred from
the negotiation and enactment of an international convention; but
it is possible that it may emerge later as a result of processes and
mechanisms unwittingly unleashed by those who first demanded international action. That is why both the enthusiast and the cynic,
in insisting on a *direct* link between international human rights activity and active value sharing, miss the point. The link, if it exists
at all, is more elusive, more indirect, and more slow to reveal itself
than those who see a new world-oriented generation about to storm
the bastions of the nationalist Establishment realize.

But some politically relevant rights are more suitable than others
in this context. Some conventions are too specific and others too
general to serve the process here summarized. I would argue that
conventions would have to meet *all* of the following requisites in
order to be ideal candidates for promoting the universal sharing of
values:[19]

(a) The right to be protected must reflect a widely shared set of
expectations among significant actors, governmental and non-governmental. These expectations need not be identical, and will not
be identical in most cases. It is enough that a large number of im-

portant actors, *for reasons peculiar to each*, comes to the conclusion that a certain right is desirable according to personal expectations. This requisite is met by all the texts listed in Table 1. But the draft Declaration on Territorial Asylum, for instance, does not meet it: though it meets the expectations of Latin American oligarchs, anti-colonial revolutionaries, and opponents of crimes against humanity, it runs counter to the expectations of traditional regimes afraid of more revolutionary neighbors and stable democracies.[20]

(b) The right to be protected must be so general in nature as to be capable of triggering activity and demands in social and economic fields close to, but not identical with, the original area of concern. That is, the right must possess a spillover capacity in order to be fully relevant to value sharing, the quality of appealing to an ever wider constituency, far beyond the original governmental and non-governmental clientele whose expectations it met. This spillover capacity ensures that the tenuous and limited consensus on which a convention may well rest initially is capable of being transcended later. Some of the conventions listed do not meet this requisite, especially the majority of the norms protected by the International Labor Code; similarly, the obligations under the UNESCO text against discrimination in education are probably too specific to qualify here.*

(c) The right to be protected must be specific enough to permit the investigation and rational evaluation of charges of violations.

---

* For the same reason this study will not consider the following texts adopted by the UN and—with a few exceptions—now in force (ratification figures as of January 1, 1969):

Suppression of the Traffic in Persons and of the Exploitation of the Prostitution of Others (1949; 39 parties)

Status of Refugees (1951; 54 parties) and additional Protocol (1967; 28 parties)

International Right of Correction (1952; 8 parties)

Political Rights of Women (1952; 61 parties)

Additional Protocol to the 1926 Slavery Convention (1953; 64 parties)

Status of Stateless Persons (1954; 19 parties) and Reduction of Statelessness (1961; 1 party)

Supplementary Convention on Slavery, etc. (1956; 73 parties)

Nationality of Married Women (1957; 41 parties)

Consent to Marriage, etc. (1962; 18 parties).

It must be specific enough to attract and appeal to a coherent and organized constituency, be it government agency or private interest group, which is willing and able to "bring charges" when violations occur. It must possess procedural specificity. This requisite is met neither by the convention against religious intolerance nor by the genocide convention; both lack sufficiently precise norms. It is doubtful that it is met in the case of the International Covenant on Civil and Political Rights in even half of the member nations of the UN.

(d) The right to be protected must be important enough to be valued by its constituency apart from and beyond the particular political context of the time and place; it must possess substantive as well as procedural specificity. Despite the diversity of regimes and polities, the right must be valued in enough nations at any one time by a specific constituency to outlive, for instance, an immediate anti-colonial or anti-fascist manifestation. If it is permanently subject to the larger political context, its legitimacy is in danger. Of all the texts listed and mentioned, only the ILO convention on freedom of association and the UN text on racial discrimination meet this requisite. In the case of freedom of association, the work of the ILO in a variety of political contexts has empirically demonstrated that this right is valued for its own sake by identifiable groups and governments; in the instance of the convention against racial discrimination, I suspect that the text will be so viewed because it happens to meet the converging interests of a large number of coherent groups all over the world. The same cannot be said to the same extent of any other international texts.

(e) The right in question must be protected by a minimum international machinery in order to be capable of the generalization specified in (b) above. This machinery must include a supervisory and an enforcement capacity; it must provide for periodic reports from member nations and afford a complaint procedure accessible not only to individuals but to organized non-governmental groups of clients as well. However, the right cannot be so controversial as to overburden the international machinery. Freedom of association and measures against racial discrimination again come closest to fitting the bill; but existing international machinery, or machinery likely to be devised in the next decade, is not capable of handling genocide charges or politically infused charges based on the provisions of the International Covenant on Civil and Political Rights.* Moreover, the reporting system now in force in the ILO is the only one that meets the requisite of a supervisory capacity.† In the absence of rights widely valued for their own sake, and without the concern of coherent client groups, it is difficult to see what effect the proposed High Commissioner for Human Rights could have as an enforcement agent. The supervisory and conciliation committees included in the freedom of association and racial discrimination texts appear more likely to be effective.

* William D. Coplin shows conclusively, for example, that the legitimacy and authority of the International Court of Justice has declined as the world has acquired more types of regimes and more diverse ideologies. He shows also that the typical and loyal client state is Western, democratic, and economically developed. The decline in authority is also associated with an increase in the political importance of the cases heard ("The World Court in the International Bargaining Process," in Robert W. Gregg and Michael Barkun, eds., *The United Nations System and Its Functions* [Princeton, N.J.: Van Nostrand, 1968], pp. 322–27). Further, a recent study by the UN Institute for Training and Research shows that 48 of 218 states ratifying five major UN human rights texts did so with the reservation that they would not submit disputes arising under the treaties to the jurisdiction of the ICJ (UNITAR, "Acceptance of Human Rights Treaties," UN doc. A/CONF. 32/15, 28 March 1968, p. 12).

† The system of periodic reports on human rights under the UN leaves a great deal to be desired; yet it is the only system now functioning, apart from the ILO's. During the first three-year period, 50 per cent of the members returned reports, during the second year 67 per cent, during the third 60 per cent, and during the most recent period only 20 per cent. Some reports arrive two years after the deadline. Few contain material from which the real sweep of human rights can be judged, being confined to texts of laws, decrees, and constitutional provisions intermixed with a little political propaganda and a few production statistics. See "Periodic Reports of Human Rights," prepared by the Secretary-General for the Commission on Human Rights, UN doc. E/CN. 4/916 and E/CN. 4/860, 1966 and 1963, respectively.

Still, it has been suggested that the reporting system, despite its acknowledged imperfections, has certain side benefits. It forces the reporting government to examine the practices of its various ministries and administrative units and at least to attempt to collect something like systematic statistics on its degree of fidelity to UN norms. In this sense, the reporting system may help sensitize a government to issues at home that normally command low priority.

In short, our paradigm of the expected effectiveness of the international protection of human rights as an agent of global value sharing suggests that only two current conventions are likely to be effective. One of these just entered into force. The other has had a life of 19 years in which all the requisites have been met. The ILO system for protecting freedom of association is our case study for showing whose rights have been successfully protected at whose expense. It is the only extant case for showing the effectiveness of the international machinery *under conditions optimal for value sharing*.[21] Surely, what cannot be achieved under this system, so long neglected by legal scholars and political analysts, is hardly likely to be achieved by other organizations or by the UN.

2. The ILO and the Protection of Human Rights

Since 1919 the ILO has been a forum for the elaboration of legal texts designed to protect industrial and agricultural workers, commercial employees, seamen, and fishermen. The conditions against which protection was to be afforded range from radiation-induced health hazards and excessively heavy packages to long working hours for women, trade union repression, and forced labor. Each text is negotiated laboriously. ILO membership includes democracies, communist and fascist dictatorships, old-fashioned military autocracies and modernizing ones, countries just emerging from tribal politics, and the most advanced industrial nations of the world. The tripartite formula of representation ensures the participation of national and international trade union and employer associations as well as governments. Moreover, the principle of public accountability is written into the norm-creating procedure: member nations must report annually, indicating whether or not they have presented labor conventions to the "competent authorities" for ratification, the reasons for non-ratification, if necessary, and the action taken to put ratified conventions into effect. These reports are minutely analyzed by a standing Committee of Experts on the Application of Conventions and Recommendations, which can and does request remedial action when the reports suggest imperfect implementation. If remedial action is not taken, the committee refers the matter to the annual International Labor Conference, whose own Committee on Application may use the ultimate sanction available: placement of the recalcitrant member nation on a "blacklist" of uncooperative states.[1]

However, of the 120 conventions that make up the International Labor Code, only two have a complaint procedure that goes beyond the annual reporting and follow-up system: the Convention Concerning Freedom of Association and Protection of the Right to Organize (No. 87, 1948) and the Right to Organize and Collective Bargaining Convention (No. 98, 1949).[2] Unique to these conventions is a *permanent* and *standing* complaint machinery that can be used *only* by non-governmental organizations of workers and employers, national and international. There is no provision in the two complaint and investigation procedures written into the ILO Constitution for standing machinery, even though the ILO is authorized to deal with alleged violations of any of its conventions. One of those procedures—in the form of "representations"—can be used only by trade unions; it was invoked with little success a dozen times between 1920 and 1938, and has not been used since. The other—in the form of "complaints"—permits one member state to direct charges of non-implementation against another; it was not invoked until 1961, when two celebrated cases involving Portugal made their appearance.[3] Apart from the fact that these procedures have not found favor in the eyes of many governments and unions, most of the conventions they cover do not meet the requisites for the progressive sharing of important values.

This is not the case with respect to the two conventions on freedom of association and collective bargaining. The crucial provision of Convention 87—the Convention Concerning Freedom of Association and Protection of the Right to Organize—is that "workers and employers, without distinction whatsoever, shall have the right to establish and, subject only to the rules of the organization concerned, to join organizations of their own choosing without previous authorization" (Article 2). Public interference of any kind with the formation and continued operation of associations is forbidden, and this applies to units at the local, municipal, regional, national, and international levels. Organization is defined broadly to include any interest group other than the military and the police (Articles 9, 10). Member states must "take all necessary and appropriate measures to ensure that workers and employers may exercise freely the right to organize" (Article 11). The only possible remaining loophole is the provision that the rights guaranteed must be practiced within the law of the land, though national law "shall not be such as to impair . . . the guarantees" (Article 8).

Convention 98—the Right to Organize and Collective Bargaining Convention—is a supplement to Convention 87, protecting workers in their jobs against anti-union discrimination: workers cannot be punished or penalized for organizing or participating in unions, or for engaging in collective bargaining. This text does not formally recognize closed or union shops, but it is so drawn as to be acceptable to countries that have such institutions.

These texts say nothing about a complaint procedure, however. Nor do they suggest that non-ratifying states are bound by their provisions. The complaint procedure that evolved came about without formal conventional or constitutional sanction. It resulted from an agreement negotiated by the ILO with the UN Economic and Social Council in 1950 setting up a Fact-Finding and Conciliation Commission. This commission was to settle disputes over the implementation of Conventions 87 and 98. However, it could not assume jurisdiction over a case unless a defendant government expressly agreed, and Peru, the first government to become the victim of a trade union complaint, refused to do so. Thereupon, the Governing Body of the ILO created a standing tripartite committee— the Committee on Freedom of Association—mandating it to examine complaints to determine whether they merited investigation and eventual referral to the Fact-Finding and Conciliation Commission. Within a few months this committee, acting on behalf of the Governing Body, in effect became the parent commission, hearing and disposing of the complaints that began arriving in large numbers. The legal basis of the committee's work, then, is the UN-ILO agreement, together with the internal Standing Orders adopted by the Governing Body and amended occasionally thereafter. Moreover, the committee has successfully asserted that all ILO members are subject to its jurisdiction *sine die*, whether or not they have ratified the conventions under its protection; the legal basis for this claim is the ILO Constitution and the appended Declaration of Philadelphia (1944), which are interpreted to mean that member states are obliged to foster freedom of association.[4]

The Committee on Freedom of Association is made up of nine members of the Governing Body, three government delegates, three employer representatives, and three worker representatives. The members, though they may be lawyers, diplomats, industrialists, or labor leaders by profession, serve in a political capacity, i.e., as representatives of organized groups: they are "politicians" by role and "experts" only incidentally. The committee received 545 separate complaints of violations of freedom of association between 1950 and the beginning of 1968.* The nature of the complaints stretches the meaning of freedom of association very far indeed: we find instances of suppression of unions through murder, arrest,

---

* The main source for this study is the body of reports on these cases. I have used Reports 1–103, published early in 1968 as "Report of the Committee on Freedom of Association," in the ILO *Official Bulletin*. Of these 545 cases, I used 486 for my statistical study. Many of the unused cases are unsuitable for tabulation and coding because insufficient detail has been revealed by the ILO: the Committee on Freedom of Association has adopted a policy of non-revelation in order to give the parties time to settle quietly or to provide an unofficial cooling-off period; only when it becomes clear that such a settlement will not be forthcoming are the full details published. Hence many of the more recent cases are still pending in the earliest stages of the procedure. In some instances cases were joined with identical complaints. A few cases could not be used because more than one defendant was named. These are the cases excluded from the tabulations: 36 (Saudi Arabia), 39 (Bolivia), 43 (Chile), 122 (Venezuela), 95 (U.S.), 123 (E. Germany), 141 (Chile), 154 (Chile), 162 (U.K.), 164 (U.S.), 201 (unknown), 203 (Hungary), 218 (unknown), 226 (Haiti), 242 (France), 281 (Belgium), 297 (USSR), 304 (Peru, South Africa, Spain, Iran), 322 (Sierra Leone), 329 (Cuba), 356 (Spain), 384 (Ecuador), 386 (India), 387 (Vietnam), 390 (Venezuela), 391 (Ecuador), 395 (Colombia), 400 (Spain), 404 (South Africa), 409 (Bolivia), 410 (Paraguay), 425 (Cuba), 434 (Colombia), 437 (Congo-K.), 446 (Panama), 470 (Greece), 473 (Ecuador), 482 (unknown), 488 (Belgium), 493 (India), 508 (Greece), 509 (Spain), 510 (Paraguay), 521 (U.K.), 522 (Dominican Republic), 523 (Canada), 524 (Morocco), 530 (Uruguay), 531 (Panama), 532 (unknown), 533 (unknown), 534 (Colombia), 537 (Indonesia), 538 (unknown), 539 (El Salvador), 540 (Spain), 541 (unknown), 542 (unknown), 543 (unknown).

and deportation; strike-breaking; restrictive and discriminatory compulsory registration procedures; rigged elections; suppression of union newspapers; seizure of union halls and union funds; discriminatory subsidization; and the persecution of political leaders who are unionists. Since the line between trade union freedom and the freedom to vote, write, speak, and peaceably assemble is very thin, the work of the committee is fertile ground for inquiring how successfully and how far the international protection of one strategically placed legal right can be pushed.

The remarkable consistency and energy of this committee is in no small measure explained by the character of its membership. From the outset, the committee has clearly been dominated by Western conceptions of trade union and political rights. India is the only Afro-Asian country that has had a government delegate; the only other non–West European governments that have been represented are Argentina, Brazil, Colombia (one term each), and Mexico (three terms). With three government seats on the committee, 18 governments could have been represented once during the six three-year terms so far available; in fact only seven governments have been, with France, India, Italy, and Mexico accounting for 15 of the available seats. The French government delegate was the committee's chairman for the first ten years; the Italian representative has been chairman ever since.

The same is true on the employer side. The head of the ILO Employers' Group has been a member of the committee since 1951. Of the nine additional employers who have served (of 18 possible incumbents), all but three have come from economically developed nations in Europe and Latin America; the only "non-capitalist employer" who served came from the United Arab Republic. On the worker side, only unions generally identified with Western positions and the International Confederation of Free Trade Unions (ICFTU) have been represented. Eight persons filled the 18 terms available; workers from four countries alone—Switzerland, Mexico, the Philippines, and the Netherlands—served 15 of them. It should be added that most of the worker and employer representatives also function as important figures in their respective international, non-governmental organizations, all of which are Western in orientation. Of the six committee members who must be deemed the most important, four come from West European countries.* No representative of a communist member nation or of a communist non-governmental organization has served; no Africans have served as regular members, though one or two are now substitutes. Given this institutional, ideological, and geographical bias toward Western values, we may well wonder to what extent the decisions of the committee succeed in shaping new norms of national conduct in the socialist camp and the Third World.

FREEDOM OF ASSOCIATION AND VALUE SHARING: SOME HYPOTHESES

I wish to use the experience of the committee, as represented by its case law, to see if the effort to define and protect trade union freedom can teach us some lessons about the international sharing of important political values. Certain specific hypotheses are developed to guide the analysis of this material. These hypotheses have been deliberately couched in such terms as to tie in with the functional model of "optimal relevance" developed in Chapter 1. They have been phrased affirmatively so as to bear out the assertions and projections explicit in that model; our data will soon show us whether behavior in fact conforms with model-derived expectation. Moreover, these hypotheses focus deliberately on a single important theme: international value sharing is likely to be enhanced to the extent that autonomous private interest groups all over the world are enabled to make use of an international protection machinery to achieve their socioeconomic and political objectives at the expense of hostile governments, *provided* that the objectives of these interest groups are similar enough and general enough to mesh with the norms proclaimed in the international machinery.

* They are Pierre Waline (employer, France: six terms), Paul Ramadier (government, France: four terms), Roberto Ago (government, Italy: three terms), and Jean Möri (worker, Switzerland: six terms). A. Sánchez-Madariaga (worker, Mexico: four terms) and M. Ghayour (employer, Iran: four terms) are the only non-Europeans with long tenure.

The logic underlying our hypotheses will be developed in greater detail when we present the data. At the moment, the hypotheses are stated tersely for the reader's convenience, grouped under three major rubrics: authority and legitimacy of international norms, types of complainants and defendants, implementation of international decisions.

Hypotheses dealing with the authority and legitimacy of international norms

1. International conventions dealing with human rights enjoy more authority and legitimacy than do other kinds of international labor conventions.

2a. International labor conventions are most legitimate and authoritative in reconciliation polities with mixed economic institutions and developed economies; they are least legitimate and authoritive in totalitarian and authoritarian polities with socialist or capitalist institutions and underdeveloped economies. Such conventions enjoy increasing authority and legitimacy in incipient reconciliation polities with growing economies.

2b. International conventions dealing with human rights show an exaggerated tendency toward high or low legitimacy and authority, as compared with other conventions, in all types of nations.

3. Over time, complaining trade unions will concentrate less and less on issues with world political implications and will focus instead on immediate issues of human rights at the national level.

Hypotheses dealing with the attributes of complainants and of defendants

4. Over time, fewer trade union Internationals will appear as complainants as their place is taken by national unions.

5. Over time, trade union Internationals representing democratic unions will be more successful than other Internationals in securing favorable ILO decisions.

6. Trade union Internationals complain most frequently of violations of basic human rights *not* tied to the world political context (Cold War and decolonization).

7. Over time, the identity of the most frequently accused defendant states will change: at first, the major actors in the Cold War and in the decolonization struggle appeared as defendants; later, mobilization, authoritarian, and oligarchical polities with underdeveloped economies will dominate the docket.

8. Over time, mobilization, authoritarian, and oligarchical nations will be accused increasingly of violating human rights in the purely local context of demands for more mass participation in economic decision-making and social reform; reconciliation polities with developed and growing economies will be accused increasingly of violating trade union rights of restricted and functionally specific scope.

9. The most severely adverse decisions are addressed to mobilization and authoritarian regimes.

10. Over time, convictions dealing with general human rights will increase most dramatically in frequency; convictions dealing with Cold War and decolonization issues will decline; convictions dealing with specific trade union issues will remain the same.

Hypotheses dealing with the severity and the implementation of ILO decisions

11a. Over time the decisions of the ILO will become increasingly critical and severe with respect to the practices of defendant nations.

11b. Over time, the decisions of the ILO will show more concern with general human rights and less with specific trade union grievances.

12. Over time, a growing number of defendants will implement adverse decisions.

13. Adverse decisions are always most readily implemented by reconciliation and insecure authoritarian and oligarchical

regimes; stable authoritarian and oligarchical regimes gradually implement more adverse decisions; mobilization regimes almost never implement adverse decisions.

14. Adverse decisions are most readily implemented by defendant nations when prosecuted jointly or simultaneously by several trade union Internationals.

15. Adverse decisions are implemented most frequently if the complaint arose in a functionally specific and narrow "trade union" context; they are implemented least frequently if the context is highly politicized through links with the Cold War and the decolonization struggle.

THE VARIABLES AND THE HYPOTHESES

We are concerned with six major clusters of material: the decisions made by the committee, the degree to which defendant governments carry out decisions, the characteristics of the defendants, the type of issues implicit in the complaints, the identity of the complainants, and the characteristics of the international system at the time the complaints are made. In the subsequent analysis, most of these variables will be paired with each other in order to verify some of the hypotheses; but the major thrust of our analytical purpose demands that we use committee decisions and government implementation as the dependent variables, and system characteristics (time), complainants, issues, and defendants as the independent variables. We now turn to a fuller description of each variable and an explanation of the method of coding.

Committee Decisions. Technically, of course, the decisions of the committee are merely recommendations addressed to the Governing Body, which are ultimately to be passed on to the accused governments for consideration. Nobody is legally bound to follow the recommendations. The committee has these options: it can dismiss a complaint out of hand, without communicating with the defendant government; it can dismiss after making inquiries via correspondence (oral proceedings are not part of the procedure); it can dismiss with a recommendation to the government to review certain practices; it can find the allegation true *and* a violation of the two texts and can recommend "changes in law and practice" to the governments, in effect rendering a verdict of guilty; and, finally, it can go beyond such a finding and recommend more severe steps, which I label sanctions.

There are four grounds for dismissal: lack of evidence; lack of jurisdiction because the complainant is not a trade union or an employers' association, or is one of these but has no direct interest in the case; lack of grounds for action because the alleged violations have been remedied or have been overtaken by events or have become irrelevant; lack of a "trade union issue" in the facts as alleged. The last point calls for further comment. Acts of persecution that do not clearly discriminate against unions are held by the committee to be "political," and hence not under its jurisdiction. But where does one draw the line? Are trade union demonstrations and strikes designed to aid a nationalist party in a colonial setting political acts? Is their suppression a violation of trade union rights? The committee has not always given consistent answers. In fact, if we wish to study how a specific norm can gradually be escalated into a general obligation, spreading from a coherent and committed constituency to a wider group, we must consider closely when and how cases are dismissed on political grounds.

Dismissals accompanied by recommendations to review questionable practices are thinly veiled warnings. The committee chooses to observe many of the diplomatic niceties of a former age, and many cases involving real violations (it is impossible to determine how many) are disguised through this formula, in the hope of obtaining ready and quiet government compliance. Judging by the committee's reports to the Governing Body, this technique is quite successful, but it is impossible to adduce supporting figures.

The committee's strongest weapon, sanctions, can take any of several forms: referral to ECOSOC, referral to the UN Secretary-General, referral to the Fact-Finding and Conciliation Commission, referral to ad hoc investigatory bodies that will visit the defendant country, or publication by the Governing Body of a report sharply critical of the defendant. But whatever their form, sanctions are confined to unfavorable publicity.

The coding of cases provided no difficulty, since my categories are identical with the official categories used by the committee. In the event of different rulings on separate allegations in a single case, the most severe was used.

Implementation. The only unambiguous information about a defendant government's follow-through on a committee decision is contained in the report of the committee, which occasionally will refer to a case in which the requested changes were made. But normally no such information is available. For the most part, we had to make our own determination, using other primary sources and secondary sources—including informants—to discover whether a given practice had been altered or a law repealed. In some cases it was possible to deduce non-implementation from the fact that the same violation continued to be brought to the committe's attention year after year, or from complaints of noncooperation in the committee's reports and other *obiter dicta*. However, the coding retains uncertainties, and less confidence attaches to the conclusions on implementation than in the case of our other variables. Substantial compliance with a request to change law and practice was coded as "great improvement," partial compliance (a frequent occurrence) as "some improvement," and the absence of any evidence of change as "no improvement."

Time Period, or "System." The principle used to arrive at a periodization of our cases is the clustering of power in the international system. But in classifying historical periods according to the relative international distribution of power, we must bear in mind two aspects of that elusive notion power. We must specify the kinds of power we mean, e.g., nuclear capability, conventional military capability, economic-industrial capacity, the ability to launch effective ideological, propaganda, or subversive offensives. We must then ask ourselves whether these kinds of power were distributed symmetrically, heterosymmetrically, or asymmetrically among the actors. A period in which all kinds of power are so distributed as to permit two actors or two blocs to share them about evenly is one of symmetry. A period in which some third force is capable of reducing the ability of the major blocs to maneuver freely on the international stage in *equal proportions* is one of heterosymmetry. And a period in which a third force (or forces) can reduce the maneuverability of the major blocs in *unequal proportions* is one of asymmetry.

Further, we must specify how these kinds of power are clustered around poles or into blocs. When single states lead or dominate (through alliances or otherwise) large segments of the globe, we speak of a polar distribution. Bipolar from 1947 until 1955 and tripolar in the immediate aftermath of the Bandung Conference, the distribution has been multipolar since the mass entrance of African nations into the world community. Note that this multipolarity implied the introduction of a heterosymmetrical distribution of power, *even though* the third force had neither the nuclear nor the conventional military capability to cut into the blocs carved out by the United States and the Soviet Union. Here, symmetry was destroyed because of the ideological-subversive capability of the third bloc and because of its ability to make claims on the economic-industrial capacity of the large powers.

Our cases were assigned to a period according to date of filing, though they often dragged on into one or two succeeding periods.[5]

Complainants. In the ILO's procedure for protecting freedom of Association, only trade unions or employer associations with an interest in the case are accepted as *bona fide* complainants; but in practice, complaints by employer associations have been confined to one or two cases. Over the last few years peasant associations in Latin America have begun to file complaints, and since these groups are affiliated with trade union Internationals, the committee accepts their cases. Complaints originating with student groups, political parties, "action committees," and the like are not accepted; neither are the very frequent complaints brought by a national trade union against a foreign government. We have coded complainants into these categories: the World Federation of Trade Unions (communist) and its international departments and regional organizations; the ICFTU (socialist democratic and reformist) and its associated trade secretariats and regional organizations; the International Federation of Christian Trade Unions

(Catholic and Protestant) and its affiliated trade secretariats and regional organizations;* national trade unions (irrespective of affiliation) complaining against their own governments; national trade unions (irrespective of affiliation) complaining against foreign governments; "other" unions, such as unaffiliated regional groupings in Africa and the Middle East; and "joint complaints," which covers a simultaneous attack by two or more of the large Internationals against a government. When a complaint was prosecuted jointly by an International and its regional and national affiliates, the International was credited. Cases in which the identity of the complainant remained unclear were not counted.

Issues. According to our guiding paradigm and our hypotheses, we should not expect to find all issues arising in the context of trade union protection equally relevant to the sharing of values. Issues that are too specific do not lend themselves to generalized application; those that are overly politicized tend to fail because of their controversiality and dependence on a limited power base. Rather, our paradigm leads us to expect issues arising over a moderately wide and moderately controversial aspect of freedom of association to be best suited to the spread of global value sharing. Accordingly, in coding our cases, we categorized issues as Cold War–connected, as linked to the decolonization process, as narrow trade union disputes of no general political implication, or as genuine human rights issues triggered by the sufferings of trade unions. It must be stressed that, for our purposes, the subject matter of the dispute, the facts alleged by the complainants, and the legal points the committee considered relevant in a case were not important; our coding was determined by the *political context* surrounding a case, by the degree of complexity and controversiality attending it. When a case was made up of many allegations of varying controversiality, the most serious or general determined our coding. One research assistant and the author together coded all the cases.

Some examples may illustrate the coding system. Assume the following: workers are arrested, union meetings are canceled, and

* This organization will be referred to as IFCTU in the text, though it recently changed its name to World Democratic Labor Movement.

the union meeting halls are closed down. If such an event occurred in Poland in 1956 and the complainant was the ICFTU or the IFCTU, it was coded as a "Cold War issue"; if the event had occurred in Italy in 1951 and the WFTU was the complainant, it too was coded as a "Cold War issue." But if the event had occurred in Aden in 1964 and the complaint was brought by several national unions that doubled as political organizations, the event was coded as a "decolonization issue," if in Brazil in 1964 in the context of the military coup and of interference with civil liberties generally, as a "human rights issue," and if anywhere in the world during a strike by a single union in a single town, in a setting of general violence but without evidence of a national policy of union repression, as a "trade union issue." Cold War– and decolonization-connected cases are unlikely to lead to value sharing; trade union issues do not tend to promote more comprehensive values. Human rights issues, however, are central to our concern.

Characteristics of defendants. One of the main weaknesses of studies of human rights is the tendency to ignore the characteristics of the nations that are supposed to ratify and enforce internationally defined norms. Each of our defendant governments—87 in all—was coded by type of political regime, by degree of economic development, and by the nature of the prevailing economic institutions. These three sets of characteristics were then combined to assign each country to a composite type. A case was credited to a composite type, or cluster, according to its date of origin. Provision was made for changes in regime and institutions, as well as for development: later complaints against the same country were credited to a different cluster, if the facts warranted, so that our 87 defendant countries appear as 118 "defendant types."[6]

The key types of polity are reconciliation regimes, mobilization regimes, authoritarian regimes, modernizing oligarchies, traditional oligarchies, and modernizing autocracies. A reconciliation regime has values that are preponderantly instrumental; its authority structure is pyramidal; its government has extensive data on the society and the economy, and uses little coercion against either. Norms are sanctioned by the constitution and by custom, history serves as a symbolic referent, integration is achieved by a bureaucracy working closely with private groups, and national identity rests on the satisfaction of the populace, which is participant in character. Government is highly accountable, elites are recruited on the basis of individual skill and merit as well as on the basis of access, enforcement of norms is flexible, resource allocation is based on market forces or on wide consultation with private enterprise, and consent groups are co-opted into the governing structure.

A mobilization regime is the exact opposite. Consummatory values predominate and the authority structure is hierarchical. A single "party" serves as the source of norms and the integrative mechanism. A "political religion" provides the symbolic referent and national identity. There is little accountability, recruitment into the elite rests on loyalty to the party, norms are rigidly enforced, resources are allocated according to a plan, and consent groups are manipulated. All national energies are "mobilized" to achieve dramatic and rapid modernization.

Authoritarian regimes are milder and more relaxed forms of mobilization regimes; sometimes they emerge after a harassed populace has succeeded in overthrowing a mobilization regime that failed to plan and manipulate consent groups successfully. Authoritarian regimes center around the person of a "presidential monarch"—an "elected ruler," civilian or military, who claims legitimacy on the basis of popular acclaim but who surrounds himself with the trappings of a court and may have come to power as the result of a coup. Instrumental values dominate, but the authority structure tends to be hierarchical; moderate amounts of coercion are used. The president himself attempts to be the source of new, modernizing, and progressive norms; he seeks to shape a new tradition, using a single party and a bureaucracy as the integrative device. National identity rests on the people's identification with the new tradition, and also on the degree of satisfaction they experience. Personal merit and skill are important in recruitment, some accountability is maintained, and norms are enforced with moderation. Though consent groups are both co-opted and manipulated, the allocation of resources is to a large extent reserved to private enterprise and mixed corporations.

A modernizing oligarchy is a regime led by a junta of dedicated civilian or military rulers, whose subjects are generally a pre-modern people only dimly aware of any formal citizenship in a state. The authority structure is hierarchical in principle, but far less efficient and rigorous in practice than in an authoritarian system. Values are consummatory at the verbal level but tend to be instrumental in practice. Formal links between the government and the society and economy are tenuous; the civil or military bureaucracy is neither large nor efficient, though committed to modernization. There is no accountability, consent groups are ignored, the enforcement of norms is rigid in principle but haphazard in practice, and recruitment to the elite rests on bureaucratic or personal identification with the ruling junta. Modernizing oligarchies have little staying power; they readily develop into authoritarian or mobilization regimes.

A traditional oligarchy, on the other hand, is a regime in which a small group of people, linked by family ties of status, controls the government, the society, and the economy; the people live in tribal or village units under traditional rules and are outside the political system altogether.

The last type of polity, the modernizing autocracy, must be included in our list, though its days are probably numbered. A modernizing autocracy is a regime headed and dominated by a traditional ruler—a king, imam, or sultan—who is determined to cajole his subjects into modernity. He seeks to use the authority he has inherited to adapt traditional norms and integrating mechanisms to the demands of social and economic modernization, and tends to rely heavily on religious authority and symbols of legitimacy to this end. The amount of political freedom he allows his subjects is conditional on the requirements of modernization and on the nature of the traditional values and structures retained—though these may easily conflict. Economic institutions and practices are being modernized (often with the assistance of foreign firms), education is stressed, and urbanization is encouraged. Clearly, traditional political norms and practices are unlikely to remain unchallenged if the socioeconomic measures undertaken bear fruit.

We have used the per capita consumption of energy to arrive

at the degree of economic development of defendant countries. This indicator is more useful than the frequently used per capita GNP index in pinpointing aspects of welfare applicable to the lower strata of society (such as trade union members) as against the total population, for per capita GNP tends to distort the benefits received where there are sharp differences in income between a very large bottom layer and a tiny top stratum, e.g., Venezuela. Energy consumption is a particularly useful indicator also where there is a large underdeveloped rural sector and a growing and mobile urban one. Rural areas do not consume much energy in household appliances; nor do new city populations concentrated in slums. Neither consumes much energy in the course of earning a living, and living standards are known to be very low, even though the aggregate GNP may not be, e.g., Japan before 1960. Moreover, energy consumption pinpoints resources devoted to industrialization. Its one weakness as an indicator is in understating the real welfare of nations engaged in successful commercial agricultural production on a large scale.

Typologies of countries rarely make provision for classifying the economic institutions, in part because there is even less agreement on the proper categories than in the case of regime types. Nevertheless, the nature of our hypotheses compels us to direct our attention to this variable. We think it likely that workers in a predominantly capitalist environment will seek the help of internationally sanctioned norms; we suspect that workers in a socialist system will not, unless they are in process of rebellion against their institutions; and we surmise that workers in systems with the attributes of the modern welfare state—neither clearly capitalistic nor clearly socialistic—will be indifferent to international protection. But we also suspect that these perceptions of interest may alter as regime and development changes trigger adaptations in the dominant economic institutions. In short, the nature of trade union and pluralist theory assigns some importance to the prevailing economic institutions. Hence, we must allow for them in our cluster of variables. Each country was assigned to one of four categories at each point in time in our periodization of the international system: capitalist, socialist, mixed, or corporatist.

TABLE 3

Profile of ILO Membership, Defendants, and Convicted Defendants, 1950–68
(in descending order of number of complaints)

Country attribute type	ILO membership[a]		Defendants[b]				Convictions		
			Countries		Complaints				
	No.	Pct.	No.	Pct.	No.	Pct.	No.	Pct. of total convictions	Pct. of complaints[c]
Reconciliation Capitalist Underdeveloped	21	12%	11	9%	72[d]	15%	22	19%	31%
Reconciliation Mixed Developed	11	6	7	6	60[e]	12	12	10	20
Reconciliation Mixed Growing	16	9	13	11	58[f]	12	9	8	16
Reconciliation Mixed Underdeveloped	15	8	14	12	57	12	10	9	18
Authoritarian Capitalist Underdeveloped	19	10	12	10	52	11	11	9	21
Modernizing autocracy Capitalist Underdeveloped	12	7	6	5	25	5	2	2	8
Traditional oligarchy Capitalist Underdeveloped	18	10	10	9	25	5	6	5	24
Authoritarian Mixed Underdeveloped	8	4	6	5	23	5	8	7	35
Not classifiable Capitalist Growing	1	1	1	1	19[g]	4	8	7	42
Reconciliation Mixed Highly developed	2	1	1	1	14[h]	3	0	0	0
Mobilization Socialist Underdeveloped	14	8	8	7	13	3	3	3	23
Authoritarian Mixed Growing	1	1	1	1	13[i]	3	4	3	31
Mobilization Mixed Underdeveloped	6	3	3	3	11	2	3	3	27
Modernizing oligarchy Capitalist Underdeveloped	7	4	5	4	11	2	2	2	18
Mobilization Socialist Growing	7	4	4	3	8	2	8	7	100

TABLE 3 (*continued*)

Profile of ILO Membership, Defendants, and Convicted Defendants, 1950–68
(*in descending order of number of complaints*)

Country attribute type	ILO membership[a]		Defendants[b]				Convictions		
			Countries		Complaints			Pct. of total convictions	Pct. of complaints[c]
	No.	Pct.	No.	Pct.	No.	Pct.	No.		
Authoritarian Corporatist Underdeveloped	3	2%	2	2%	6	1%	2	2%	33%
Modernizing oligarchy Mixed Underdeveloped	5	3	4	3	5	1	2	2	40
Authoritarian Not classifiable Underdeveloped	1	1	1	1	3	1	0	0	0
Reconciliation Capitalist Growing	2	1	1	1	2	0	0	0	0
Mobilization Capitalist Underdeveloped	4	2	2	2	2	0	2	2	100
Authoritarian Socialist Underdeveloped	2	1	2	2	2	0	1	1	50
Modernizing oligarchy Socialist Underdeveloped	1	1	1	1	2	0	0	0	0
Reconciliation Corporatist Underdeveloped	1	1	1	1	1	0	1	1	100
Modernizing oligarchy Capitalist Growing	1	1	1	1	1	0	1	1	100
Not classifiable Capitalist Underdeveloped	—	—[j]	1	1	1	0	0	0	0
Mobilization Socialist Developed	3	2	0	0	0	0	0	0	0

Note: Columns do not add to 100 per cent because of rounding on this and subsequent tables.

[a] The actual ILO membership at maximum was 120. Many countries, however, were placed in more than one type if regime, economic institutions, or economic development underwent change during the period covered.

[b] The actual number of countries appearing as defendants was 87. The number here coded is larger for the reason explained in footnote *a*.

[c] This figure represents the percentage of complaints against countries in this cluster that resulted in decisions to change law or practice involving sanctions.

[d] Of which 45 cases against Greece.   [e] Of which 48 cases against the U.K.

[f] Of which 26 cases against France.   [g] All against the Republic of South Africa.

[h] All against the U.S.   [i] All against Argentina.

[j] This refers to Rhodesia, which is not a member of the ILO. The case was originally brought against Great Britain.

ILO MEMBERSHIP AND DEFENDANTS:
A PROFILE OVER TIME

A profile of the ILO membership, of the countries appearing as defendants, and of the countries suffering "convictions" can be found in Table 3. Quite clearly, there are no startling differences between the percentage of countries grouped in each type in the entire membership and the percentage of the same types appearing as defendants; the defendants appear in roughly equal proportion to the frequency of the type in the total membership. However, the number of complaints against the various types of defendants is not equally distributed. A disproportionately large number of complaints were filed against reconciliation polities with capitalist institutions and underdeveloped economies and against reconciliation polities with mixed institutions and developed or highly developed economies. In the first instance, the disproportion results from Greece having been singled out as a defendant among the countries in its cluster; in the second, Britain and the United States, respectively, were popular targets. In the case of Britain, most of the complaints dealt with nationalist agitation in overseas territories; in the American case, the complaints were filed primarily by unions critical of special security measures adopted during the Korean War. The other two instances of marked disproportionality are explained by the monopolization by single countries—South Africa and Argentina—of two clusters of attributes; both are favorite targets of national and international trade unions.

Nor is the rate of conviction always similar to the number of complaints filed. Reconciliation regimes—Britain and Greece excepted—were not often found guilty. Some mobilization regimes were convicted with startling frequency, notably the Soviet Union, Czechoslovakia, and Poland during a phase of the Cold War. South Africa too has often been found guilty. In almost all other cases, the frequency of guilt is quite similar to the frequency of complaint. Thus, given a mean guilty score for all defendants of 24.1 per cent, the disproportionate share borne by mobilization, authoritarian, and oligarchical regimes is quite evident.

The composition of the international system has been moving

TABLE 4

Changes in ILO Membership and Defendant Profiles, 1952–68

(*per cent*)

Country attribute type[a]	1952–55		1956–60		1961–68	
	Member-ship	Defen-dant	Member-ship	Defen-dant	Member-ship	Defen-dant
Reconciliation Capitalist Underdeveloped	7%	10%	10%	7%	10%	7%
Reconciliation Capitalist Growing	0	0	0	0	2	1
Reconciliation Mixed Underdeveloped	15	26	9	11	8	13
Reconciliation Mixed Growing	13	13	13	9	9	10
Reconciliation Mixed Developed	10	3	9	7	9	7
Reconciliation Mixed Highly developed	3	3	1	2	2	1
Mobilization Capitalist Underdeveloped	0	0	0	0	3	3
Mobilization Mixed Underdeveloped	4	6	3	2	3	1
Mobilization Socialist Underdeveloped	4	0	7	7	8	6
Mobilization Socialist Growing	6	6	5	7	3	0
Mobilization Socialist Developed	1	0	1	0	3	0
Authoritarian Capitalist Underdeveloped	4	10	13	9	14	13
Authoritarian Mixed Underdeveloped	0	0	4	7	5	6
Authoritarian Corporatist Underdeveloped	3	3	3	2	1	1

continued

TABLE 4 (*continued*)

Changes in ILO Membership and Defendant Profiles, 1952–68

(*per cent*)

Country attribute type[a]	1952–55		1956–60		1961–68	
	Membership	Defendant	Membership	Defendant	Membership	Defendant
Authoritarian Socialist Underdeveloped	0%	0%	0%	0%	2%	3%
Modernizing autocracy Capitalist Underdeveloped	7	3	9	9	9	6
Modernizing oligarchy Capitalist Underdeveloped	4	6	3	2	3	4
Modernizing oligarchy Capitalist Growing	1	3	0	0	0	0
Modernizing oligarchy Mixed Underdeveloped	3	3	3	7	1	0
Traditional oligarchy Capitalist Underdeveloped	14	0	6	9	5	9
Not classifiable[b] Capitalist Growing	1	3	1	2	1	1

[a] Types never accounting for 1 per cent or less were omitted.
[b] South Africa withdrew from the ILO in 1964.

steadily toward an increasing percentage of authoritarian and mobilization regimes, ruling in economically underdeveloped countries. If we assume that most of our hypotheses are correct, these profiles suggest a clouded future for the system of protection. And since, concurrently, the percentage of reconciliation regimes with mixed institutions and growing or developed economies is declining, Table 4 suggests that, if the trend there shown continues into a new historical phase, the outlook is not good for the evolution of an authoritative, legitimate, and effective system of protecting human rights likely to stimulate value sharing.

3. Authority and Legitimacy of International Norms

International legal obligations, including norms protecting labor against a large variety of dangers and abuses, clearly vary in degree of generality and scope. The assertion that a wider sharing of values is taking place globally might mean simply that there is more agreement among nations on postal rates, on maximum weights to be lifted by longshoremen, or on the precise meaning of terms in the pharmacopeia. It is therefore essential to distinguish between broadly based norms that will enhance human freedom, and obligations that promote convenience or well-being without in any sense implying a rapprochement among varying cultures or ideologies. If we then affirm that human rights conventions are more legitimate and more authoritative than other and more specific types of conventions, we should be able to detect a progressive sharing of international values relating to human rights. This leads us to our first hypothesis.

Hypothesis I. International conventions dealing with human rights enjoy more authority and legitimacy than do other kinds of international labor conventions.

Much depends here on how we define and measure the elusive concepts of legitimacy and authority. Legitimacy means that nations demand, invoke, *and subject themselves* voluntarily to new norms in a field they consider important. Hence the extent to which international conventions are accepted, i.e., ratified, after laborious, multilateral negotiations is a fair measure of legitimacy. We computed an "acceptance score" by dividing the actual ratification figure for groups of all ILO conventions by the number of conventions that could have been ratified by each country.[1] We then did the same computation for seven ILO "human rights" conventions.* Authority I define as the capacity of an international organization to compel or persuade a member nation to carry out its obligations despite that nation's reluctance to do so. To measure this dimension we adapted a scale developed by E. A. Landy and contrasted the same two sets of conventions. The "conformity" scale measures the frequency (or fidelity) with which nations carry into their domestic law and practice the international norms they formally ratified. The conformity score is computed by contrasting the number of critical observations addressed to member states by the ILO Committee of Experts with the number of ratifications.[2] In addition, a more drastic measure of authority was devised: an "implementation score" that measures the frequency with which countries improve their performance as a result of ILO criticism. Full implementation was scored more heavily than partial implementation, and the sum was divided by the number of critical observations. Member nations were not debited with denunciations of conventions they frequently violated (though these occur occasionally).[3] The legitimacy and authority of ILO conventions from 1927 to 1964 are as follows:

	Acceptance	Conformity	Implementation
All conventions (100)	.26	.70	.42
Human rights conventions (7) ...	.61	.73	.22

As the acceptance scores show, human rights in ILO texts are dramatically more legitimate than other kinds of international labor norms. However, a comparison with the acceptance of UN human rights texts fails to bear out this finding.[4] Ratification scores were computed for ILO members serving on the UN Commission

* The human rights conventions are: 11 (Freedom of Association, Agriculture), 29 (Forced Labor), 87 (Freedom of Association and Protection of the Right to Organize), 98 (Right to Organize and Collective Bargaining), 100 (Equal Remuneration for Men and Women), 105 (Abolition of Forced Labor), and 111 (Discrimination, Employment, and Occupation).

on Human Rights in 1968, i.e., nations presumably with a special interest in the international protection of human rights. Only four countries (France, Israel, Sweden, Yugoslavia) had ratified half or more of the available texts; most of the nations had become party to less than five of 16 completed treaties.

When it comes to authoritativeness, the picture is even cloudier. Both kinds of ILO conventions score well with respect to the conformity of domestic legislation and practice with ILO norms. But both kinds score much worse with respect to the correction of violations, with the implementation score for human rights conventions only half as good as the overall implementation score! In short, the special authority of human rights conventions is far from established in international practice.

The total picture must be broken down so that we can determine what type of nation is most (or least) receptive to the sharing of norms. Conventional wisdom suggests that reconciliation regimes should be more interested in the welfare of their populations than other types of regimes. Economic history suggests that countries with some penchant toward economic planning and social welfare legislation should be more receptive to international norms tending to equalize the conditions of world competition than purely capitalistic countries, which might be expected to exploit low labor costs in world trade. Thus:

Hypothesis 2a. International labor conventions are most legitimate and authoritative in reconciliation polities with mixed economic institutions and developed economies; they are least legitimate and authoritative in totalitarian and authoritarian polities with socialist or capitalist institutions and underdeveloped economies. Such conventions enjoy increasing authority and legitimacy in incipient reconciliation polities with growing economies.

Our goal here is to pinpoint differences—if any—between the legitimacy and authoritativeness of general obligations and the legitimacy and authoritativeness of texts designed to protect broad human rights. Paying due regard to the imputed motives of rulers, employers, and administrators, we should expect to find a regime or an economy anxious to improve welfare in general espe-

TABLE 5

Legitimacy and Authority of ILO Conventions for Selected Types of Member States

Attribute[a]	Number of countries	All conventions, 1927-64			Number of countries	Human rights conventions, 1948-64		
		Accept	Conform	Implement		Accept	Conform	Implement
Reconciliation	28	.32	.75	.53	36	.63	.82	.32
Mobilization	8	.21	.84	.20[b]	16	.76	.72	.18
Authoritarian	14	.19	.84	.40	15	.61	.66	.07
Modernizing autocracy	0	—	—	—	5	.54	.92	.50[c]
Capitalist	42	.16	.75	.31	42	.55	.72	.25
Mixed	5	.43	.61	.45[d]	32	.67	.84	.27
Socialist	5	.25	.90	.25[b]	12	.80	.64	.14[c]
Underdeveloped	69	.19	.70	.34	69	.59	.75	.21
Growing	6	.35	.77	.59[d]	8	.57	.92	.50[c]
Developed	0	—	—	—	5	.69	.90	.17[b]

[a] Scores were calculated only for those attributes that showed a *stable* population of at least five identical countries for the entire period.
[b] For three countries only.
[c] For two countries only.
[d] For five countries only.
[e] For eight countries only.

cially interested in protecting human rights, and conversely, a regime or an economy indifferent to measures designed to improve welfare even more indifferent to the acceptance of generalized human rights norms. Therefore:

Hypothesis 2b. International conventions dealing with human rights show an exaggerated tendency toward high or low legitimacy and authority, as compared with other conventions, in all types of nations.

Table 5 gives some data on this score. Our information is fragmentary because there were relatively few cases in which a statistically significant number of countries retained the same attribute over the whole period covered. (Insufficient data existed for human rights conventions prior to World War II to warrant carrying the comparison back to 1927.) Nevertheless, some comment is required. Let us examine the acceptance figures in order to determine the relative degree of legitimacy among regimes. With respect to all conventions, countries with the attributes of reconciliation regimes, mixed institutions, and growing economies, certainly accept far more than the mean of .26, whereas all other countries are at or below the mean. But as far as human rights texts are concerned, these same countries score only at or close to the mean of .61! On the other hand, mobilization regimes and socialist economies accept human rights obligations far more generously than predicted. Authoritarian regimes and underdeveloped economies score below the mean for general legitimacy and just at the mean on the human rights side. Democratic and developed nations, then, are not unusually eager to accept human rights obligations, and mobilization-socialist regimes are almost reckless in this regard. In summary, Hypothesis 2a is confirmed, but Hypothesis 2b is refuted with respect to the legitimacy of international norms: the predicted relationship between type of country and an exaggerated support for (or rejection of) human rights obligations does not in fact exist.

Our linked hypotheses fare no better when we turn to the question of authority. With respect to all ILO conventions, no single category of nation performed exactly as predicted. Reconciliation polities conform and implement only slightly better than the mean performance, whereas mobilization and authoritarian polities are far more faithful to their obligations than predicted, according to the conformity figures. (The statistics for implementation should not be taken too seriously here because of the smallness of the sample.) Capitalist and socialist nations conform better than predicted, but mixed economies conform well below the mean! In short, if we seek to explain international behavior on the basis of national attributes, we have to concede that there appears to be no consistent link between good performance on the legitimacy scale and equally good behavior with respect to authority.

Nor is the authority of human rights conventions always more (or less) striking than the authority of general conventions as predicted. Reconciliation regimes do indeed conform and implement to a considerably greater degree than the mean, and authoritarian regimes show the predicted resistance. But mobilization regimes perform very near the mean on both counts, as do capitalist and underdeveloped economies; in short, they show more deference to human rights texts than suggested by our hypotheses. Mixed economies perform somewhat better than the mean, though not greatly, and socialist economies perform fully as poorly as we predicted. Growing and developed economies show the very high conformity on human rights texts that seemed appropriate for them.

Thus human rights conventions *are* more authoritative than general obligations for reconciliation regimes and growing and developed economies as compared to other regimes. As for legitimacy, mobilization and socialist countries grant more legitimacy to human rights texts (to which they then conform less often) than reconciliation and capitalist nations do. Could these countries be suspected of ratifying such texts for external propaganda purposes rather than out of a serious desire to expose themselves to a sharing of values? Certainly their implementation scores do not suggest that value sharing is much of a temptation for them, or for authoritarian regimes either.

A functional approach to the study of human rights takes for granted that international concern may first be expressed as a result of a political or ideological interest, with a text or a committee seeking to "protect" human rights serving merely as an instrument of propaganda. It assumes that the first cases to be brought to the attention of a supervisory organ will be heavily invested with global political content (e.g., part of the Cold War confrontation or an episode in a general struggle against colonial rule). But the functional approach postulates that complainants will "learn" to use the machinery for other types of issues as well. It is therefore possible that the machinery will evolve in such a way as to become a forum for very specific complaints, involving local issues of no interest to international value sharing. But it is also possible that cases involving very general human rights will grow out of an initially heavily politicized setting. Our problem, in looking into the content of the authority and legitimacy of the human rights norms, is to discover whether, over time, the ILO complaint machinery has indeed evolved from a focus on heavily politicized issues to one that stresses general human rights, without at the same time becoming so specialized as to interfere with the growth of important international values. Thus:

Hypothesis 3. Over time, complaining trade unions will concentrate less and less on issues with world political implications and will focus instead on immediate issues of human rights at the national level.

As Table 6 clearly shows, between 1950 and 1968, the right of freedom of association, guaranteed under Conventions 87 and 98, was increasingly emancipated from the context of the Cold War

TABLE 6

Freedom of Association: Incidence of Issues over Time, 1950–68

Period	Number of cases	Cold war	Decoloni- zation	Human rights	Trade union	Unclassi- fiable
1950–51	41	41%	20%	22%	15%	2%
1952–55	88	30	8	28	30	4
1956–60	91	19	5	36	30	10
1961–68	266	7	5	38	32	18
Total	486	16%	7%	35%	30%	12%

and anti-colonial struggles. Cases dealing with the general human rights implications of freedom of association grew steadily in incidence, presumably—and in full consistency with the requisites of a functional strategy—as a result of lessons learned by the complaining trade unions.

However, the functionally specific category of "trade union" issues profited from the same trend in even greater proportions. If this category continues to grow at the current rate, such issues will consume more and more of the time and energy of the ILO and the unionists working to develop a jurisprudence that will maximize the enjoyment of important rights. Though this would still benefit the workers of many countries and many industries, the issues involved in trade union cases are not broad enough to trigger general concern or promote universal principles. In short, a continuation of the trend toward extreme functional specificity will reduce the number and intensity of values that lend themselves most readily to international sharing. The trend so far has been toward the right kind of sharing; our figures make it uncertain that the trend will continue.

SUMMARY

Our objective was to delineate the degree of legitimacy and authority certain ILO and UN human rights conventions command internationally, a preliminary step in determining the extent to which governments appear to share important values regarding the freedoms of their citizens. What have we discovered?

In the aggregate, human rights norms are clearly much more legitimate than technical labor conventions. However, they are *not* more authoritative; in fact, according to our crucial indicator of following ILO criticism, they are much *less* authoritative. A closer examination of the attitudes of various types of regimes and economies has disclosed that human rights texts do not enjoy unusual legitimacy among reconciliation and authoritarian regimes, but are generously ratified by mobilization polities. Economic development does not show a striking correlation with the acceptance of human rights norms; socialist countries find them more attractive than countries with capitalist or mixed institutions. With respect to authority, however, the picture is different. As predicted, human rights texts are most authoritative for reconciliation polities with developed or growing economies and mixed economic institutions, least authoritative for mobilization regimes with socialist economies, and of indifferent interest to authoritarian regimes, capitalist institutions, and underdeveloped economies. Finally, the trend in the pattern of complaints submitted by trade unions to the ILO Governing Body since 1950 clearly shows a tendency away from highly politicized issues toward very specific trade union concerns and toward the generalizable implications of freedom of association. In sum, the total picture, though not uniformly hostile to the progressive sharing of important human values, is by no means consistently favorable to such a trend.

4. Complainants and Defendants

A functional approach to the progressive sharing of values through human rights law makes explicit assumptions about the optimal behavior organizations that seek to make use of existing international machinery to protect the rights of their members. Since knowledge of ILO procedure is not evenly diffused among the trade unions of the world, and since the strength and national power of unions varies greatly from country to country, the optimal development would see the large Internationals acting as mentors to young and struggling national trade unions, at first triggering the complaint machinery, then gradually abdicating this role in favor of their national affiliates. In so doing, the Internationals would in fact have "socialized" national unions into the international machinery and its norms, thus contributing to the international sharing of values. Furthermore, if unions devoted to democratic values and peaceful processes should prove to be more successful than totalitarian organizations in pressing their claims, the resolution of inter-group conflict by peaceful and democratic means would gain strength as an internationally shared norm. Finally, if the complainants should increasingly address themselves to genuine human rights problems, the sharing of values conducive to the protection of individual and group freedom would also be enhanced; and as a concomitant the autonomy of the interna-

TABLE 7

Shifts in the Identity of Complainants, 1950–68

Period	Number of cases	Complainant						
		ICFTU	WFTU	IFCTU	Joint international	Other international	National union v. own govt.	National union v. foreign govt.
1950–51	41	15%	58%	0%	5%	0%	12%	10%
1952–55	88	3	53	0	5	5	24	10
1956–60	91	10	27	9	10	3	33	8
1961–68	266	6	13	15	7	8	40	11
Total	486	7%	27%	10%	7%	6%	33%	10%

tional complaint machinery would be strengthened. This reasoning leads us to Hypothesis 4.

Hypothesis 4. Over time, fewer trade union Internationals will appear as complainants as their place is taken by national unions.

According to Table 7 the hypothesis is valid: a certain socialization does seem to have accompanied the national unions' initiation into a world legal procedure. We should note, however, that though the ICFTU and WFTU complaints have declined in incidence, the complaints of the IFCTU and its regional and specialized affiliates have increased sharply. This appears to be the result of a drastic radicalization of the Christian International's unions in Latin America, including their entry into the field of agricultural labor. Furthermore, complaints by the autonomous Internationals, notably in the Middle East and Africa, which shun affiliation with any of the world organizations of workers, are also rising. At the moment, it is not clear whether this increase is contributing to global value sharing, or whether it merely represents a regionalization of expectations and norms.

Hypothesis 5. Over time, trade union Internationals representing democratic unions will be more successful than other Internationals in securing favorable ILO decisions.

In our findings, the ICFTU boasted a conviction score of 57 per cent on the complaints brought, against 21 per cent for the communist WFTU and 20 per cent for the Christian IFCTU. And complaints made jointly or simultaneously by two or more of the large Internationals (an approach used in 32 cases, with the ICFTU as one party in most) had a conviction rate of 78 per cent! Meanwhile, national unions lodging complaints against their own governments scored only 20 per cent, and all other types of complainants scored even lower. Our hypothesis, in general, is confirmed. But the significance of our findings for the progressive sharing of values is problematical. The IFCTU is surely as democratic as the ICFTU, as are many of the unsuccessful national unions. Furthermore, the success of the ICFTU and its co-complainants in Geneva runs counter to the worldwide trend toward a reduced percentage of reconciliation-type regimes in which democratic and autonomous unions can flourish. Before drawing elaborate conclusions from the confirmed hypothesis, then, one would have to determine, first, whether these victories were not in fact scored against regimes already committed to democratic values and so do not imply a wider sharing of values, and, second, whether the convictions resulted in implementation. A less positive interpretation of our findings suggests simply that the ICFTU is so often successful because its leaders are also key members of the supervision and complaint machinery.

Hypothesis 6. Trade union Internationals complain most frequently of violations of basic human rights not tied to the world political context.

According to our findings, the ICFTU and the IFCTU, singly or in concert, do concentrate on human rights issues: the ICFTU brought 64 per cent of its cases in this category and the IFCTU 59 per cent. In joint actions by the Internationals, 56 per cent of the complaints were against violations of human rights outside the context of the Cold War and the decolonization struggle. The WFTU stressed the Cold War in 38 per cent of its cases and human rights in only 35 per cent. National unions bringing complaints against their own governments focused on violations of specific trade union rights in 54 per cent of their cases, whereas national unions accusing foreign governments stressed Cold War–connected issues. As far as the democratic unions are concerned, therefore, the hypothesis is clearly confirmed. Behavior under this rubric would tend to reinforce general value sharing, provided the strictures observed above concerning implementation and the survival of reconciliation-type regimes are borne in mind.

DEFENDANTS—GUILTY AND INNOCENT

This brings us, then, to another crucial dimension of our whole inquiry: what is the incidence of convictions and complaints with respect to various types of defendants? We already know that a disproportionate number of complaints was brought against reconciliation regimes with mixed economic institutions and flourishing economies, as well as against certain favorite national targets: Britain, France, Greece, Argentina, and South Africa, which together accounted for almost 35 per cent of the total number of complaints. In large part, the British and French cases arose in the decolonization context; South Africa's appearance as a defendant is, of course, due to an almost universal abhorrence of the *apartheid* policy and of the legal means used to enforce it in trade unions. However, Greece and Argentina appear frequently not because their labor practices are more repressive than those of many other countries but because the complaining unions are unusually articulate and well connected internationally. In short, since the ability and willingness of unions to complain is not randomly distributed throughout the world, access, litigiousness, and politics also play a part in the incidence of cases against certain defendants.

Again, we must ask, what trends in the evolution of the defendant population would be optimal for the development of an international consensus on human rights? It seems obvious that there is relatively little need for ILO machinery to promote individual freedoms and the rights of private groups in reconciliation regimes, where these values are already well established. On the contrary, the object of the machinery is to promote such values in mobilization, authoritarian, and oligarchical polities, where autonomous private groups do not yet function. The optimal pattern, then, would see these regimes becoming the defendants more and more often, with the most critical and severe decisions addressed to them. If such regimes were to be accused increasingly of violations of freedom of association in the local context of demands for social reform and mass participation rather than in a politicized world context, the sharing of values ought to be enhanced internationally, thanks to the exclusion of broad propaganda aims and claims; grass-roots concern for freedom is unlikely to be triggered in the Third World by generalized charges of "capitalist imperialism" or "the world communist conspiracy."

Supposing that reconciliation polities were to drop out as defendants on broad charges, they might still be the targets of complaints of violations of specific trade union rights. Such a trend would contribute to the legitimacy of the ILO machinery, though not necessarily to a broader sharing of basic values, since these issues are virtually unique to industrial countries with strong pluralistic structures. Finally, the optimal pattern would see the conviction rate show its most consistent growth in the general "human rights" area, decline in the area of Cold War and decolonization issues, and remain stable in the area of locally specific trade union issues. We must now state and test the hypotheses designed to probe this pattern.

Hypothesis 7. Over time, the identity of the most frequently accused states will change: at first, the major actors in the Cold War and decolonization struggle appeared as defendants; later, mobilization, authoritarian, and oligarchical polities with underdeveloped economies will dominate the docket.

We know from Table 6 that the greatest incidence of Cold War and decolonization disputes occurred before 1956; we also know that most authoritarian regimes and many mobilization regimes and modernizing autocracies became part of the international system after that date. In our findings only a few defendant types had as much as 20 per cent of the complaints brought against them in the combined category of Cold War and decolonization issues. Among those approximating this highly politicized context were reconciliation regimes with mixed economies, both developed and growing; about 21 per cent of their cases involved the Cold War and about 25 per cent the decolonization struggle. The score of the United States on Cold War cases is much higher, 53 per cent;

the score for underdeveloped socialist countries is also up to 53 per cent, and Eastern Europe's rises to 100 per cent. In general, then, the hypothesis is confirmed.

Hypothesis 8. Over time, mobilization, authoritarian, and oligarchical nations will be accused increasingly of violating human rights in the purely local context of demands for more mass participation in economic decision-making and social reform; reconciliation polities with developed and growing economies will be accused increasingly of violating trade union rights of restricted and functionally specific scope.

Table 8 matches the incidence of human rights and trade union issues against defendant types, rank-ordering the defendants according to their deviation from the mean incidence of human rights issues (34.6 per cent of all complaints against all defendants).

As we can see, in terms of alleged violations of human rights unconnected with global political struggles, the most frequent targets are all economically underdeveloped (except for South Africa). Most of the defendants possess capitalist economic institutions; politically, they are largely oligarchical and authoritarian. The only mobilization regimes appearing frequently are noncommunist. Reconciliation polities all score at or below mean frequency, with the underdeveloped and capitalist ones more vulnerable to complaint than the others. Mobilization regimes with socialist institutions score far below the mean only because the vigorous complaints against them, and the resulting convictions, were made in the context of the Cold War rather than in the context of human rights as such.

The contrast between the incidence and distribution of human rights complaints and the incidence and distribution of trade union rights complaints is interesting: the defendants most vulnerable to human rights complaints are least often accused of violating trade union rights. To a considerable extent this reflects the high degree of trade union politicization in developing and nondemocratic nations as compared to more "mature" union movements; often what is considered a routine union dispute in the West easily acquires the aura of a basic struggle in the Third World. Devel-

TABLE 8

Freedom of Association: Defendant Types, Human Rights, and Trade Union Issues, 1950–68

(rank-ordered according to deviation from mean incidence of human rights complaints)

Defendant type	Human rights (Mean: 34.6%)	Trade union rights (Mean: 29.8%)	Defendant type	Human rights (Mean: 34.6%)	Trade union rights (Mean: 29.8%)
Traditional oligarchy Capitalist Underdeveloped	+37	−14	Reconciliation Mixed Underdeveloped	+2	+11
Authoritarian[a] Corporatist Underdeveloped	+32	−30	Modernizing autocracy Capitalist Underdeveloped	−3	+18
Not classifiable[b] Capitalist Growing	+29	−19	Authoritarian Mixed Growing	−12	+32
Authoritarian Capitalist Underdeveloped	+25	−3	Reconciliation Mixed Growing	−17	+1
Modernizing oligarchy Capitalist Underdeveloped	+11	−12	Reconciliation Mixed Highly developed	−28	−1
Mobilization[c] Mixed Underdeveloped	+11	−21	Mobilization Socialist Underdeveloped	−28	−14
Authoritarian Mixed Underdeveloped	+5	+1	Reconciliation Mixed Developed	−30	+2
Reconciliation Capitalist Underdeveloped	+3	+1	Mobilization Socialist Growing	−30	−35

Note: Types accounting for fewer than six cases were omitted. Cases included: 467. Defendants included: 105.

[a] Portugal, Brazil (until 1950s).   [b] South Africa.   [c] Argentina (since 1965).

oped and economically growing reconciliation polities with mixed institutions score at mean level for trade union complaints; reconciliation regimes with underdeveloped economies and mixed institutions far exceed it, thus demonstrating that their trade unions are quite prepared to invoke international procedures in a fight for a larger slice of the limited welfare pie. Modernizing autocracies usually try to restrain, if not repress, voluntary organizations in their effort to make modernization compatible with traditional values and sanctions; nevertheless, their unions seem active enough to challenge them in the realm of trade union rights, if not in the riskier realm of human rights issues.

We can conclude that authoritarian and oligarchical regimes (but not mobilization regimes in large numbers) are indeed the victims of accusations challenging the ruler's right to preempt decision-making in the economic and social sectors. This is most desirable in terms of the functional logic underlying our projection of international value sharing; it would be better still if mobilization regimes and modernizing autocracies were subject to the same practice, as they apparently are not. As for the second part of our hypothesis, reconciliation regimes, far from appearing increasingly as the targets of complaints involving narrow trade union issues, are in fact not particularly prominent as targets of non-politicized complaints of any kind. Their place in the tableau of charges and decisions suggests that in this respect they are contributing little to further a concern for internationally shared values.

Hypothesis 9. The most severely adverse decisions are addressed to mobilization and authoritarian regimes.

Table 9 rank-orders the various defendant types by their "guilt score," the total percentage of adverse decisions, whether calls for changes or sanctions, rendered against them. The mean guilt score for the defendants of all types is 24 per cent of the decisions handed down.

Apart from South Africa and Argentina (under Onganía), the most severely judged countries are certainly mobilization and authoritarian regimes. In the cases against the Eastern European na-

TABLE 9

Freedom of Association: Defendant Types and Adverse Decisions, 1950–68

Defendant type	Number of defendants in type	Number of complaints	Number of convictions	Number of convicted defendants	Adverse decisions as pct. of complaints
Mobilization Socialist Growing	4	8	8	4[a]	100%
Not classifiable Capitalist Growing	1	19	8	1[b]	42
Authoritarian Mixed Underdeveloped	6	23	8	3[c]	35
Authoritarian Corporatist Underdeveloped	2	6	2	2[d]	33
Authoritarian Mixed Growing	1	13	4	1[e]	31
Reconciliation Capitalist Underdeveloped	11	72	22	7[f]	31
Mobilization Mixed Underdeveloped	3	11	3	2[g]	27
Traditional oligarchy Capitalist Underdeveloped	10	25	6	3[h]	24
Mobilization Socialist Underdeveloped	8	13	3	2[i]	23
Authoritarian Capitalist Underdeveloped	12	52	11	8[j]	21
Reconciliation Mixed Developed	7	60	12	2[k]	20
Modernizing oligarchy Capitalist Underdeveloped	5	11	2	2[l]	18
Reconciliation Mixed Underdeveloped	14	57	10	6[m]	18
Reconciliation Mixed Growing	13	58	9	3[n]	16

TABLE 9 (*continued*)

Freedom of Association: Defendant Types and Adverse Decisions, 1950–68

Defendant type	Number of defendants in type	Number of complaints	Number of convictions	Number of convicted defendants	Adverse decisions as pct. of complaints
Modernizing autocracy Capitalist Underdeveloped	6	25	2	2[o]	8%
Reconciliation Highly developed Mixed	1	14	0	0[p]	0

Types accounting for fewer than six cases (or 1 per cent of complaints) were omitted. The defendants involved were Burma, Congo (B), Somalia, Sudan (under Abboud regime), Ghana (after Nkrumah), Brazil (second Vargas regime), Venezuela (under Pérez Jiménez).

[a] U.S.S.R., Poland, Hungary, Czechoslovakia.
[b] South Africa.
[c] Bolivia, Turkey, Spain.
[d] Portugal, Spain.
[e] Argentina.
[f] Chile, Colombia, Dominican Republic, Greece, Japan, Peru, Singapore.
[g] Argentina, Guatemala.
[h] Burundi, Ecuador, Paraguay.
[i] Cuba, Syria.
[j] Cuba, Dahomey, Guatemala, Honduras, Liberia, Senegal, Uganda, Upper Volta.
[k] Canada, U.K.
[l] Jordan, Venezuela.
[m] Brazil, Chile, Colombia, Costa Rica, Uruguay, Pakistan.
[n] France, Argentina, Chile.
[o] Libya, Thailand.
[p] U.S.

tions, all lodged during the loose bipolar and tripolar phases of the international system, the guilt score reflects merely the Cold War tensions of the time. More interesting and suggestive are the judgments pronounced against Bolivia, Spain (since 1960), and Turkey, as well as the judgments against Portugal and Spain (before 1960). Indeed, authoritarian regimes, which are not always insistent on having their way, since their ideological commitments are somewhat flexible, may be likely candidates for carrying out adverse international decisions.

Also interesting is the large number of reconciliation regimes in the earlier stages of economic development that are "guilty" above the mean. Most of them are committed, at some rhetorical level, to civil liberties and progressive social legislation. However, the power of the government is sometimes not very extensive, and internal opposition to these commitments may be strong. Sometimes the danger of an insurgent movement linked to trade unionism persuades a government to take repressive measures against certain unions despite a commitment to civil liberties, as witness Singapore today and Chile in the early 1950s.

It is not surprising that reconciliation regimes with growing and developed economies were not often found guilty; in fact, the only Western, developed democracies so adjudged were France, Canada, and Britain. On the other hand, we might have expected authoritarian nations with capitalist institutions, such as most African and Central American nations, to be convicted more often than they were. The same expectation attaches to modernizing autocracies in Asia and Africa; yet only Libya and Thailand were convicted. The committee was long disposed to dismiss complaints alleging violations of trade union rights when the context involved local revolutionary activity; as a consequence, Latin American governments often avoided adverse decisions in the early years, but the trend is toward more stringent condemnations of essentially similar practices in Africa.

All in in all, it is difficult to avoid the conclusion that adverse decisions have fallen very heavily on Latin American and African countries, and on some Asian nations, not to mention the severe judgments, including sanctions, against the Warsaw Pact bloc. We are not suggesting that the situations the ILO found condemnable did not exist; but we suspect that there were restrictions on free trade unionism elsewhere (in India, Iran, Pakistan under Ayub, Mexico, and Yugoslavia, for example) that could have been judged less leniently, if the committee had been of somewhat different composition. Hence the confirmation of the hypothesis may not mean much; it must yet be tested against our data on implementation. One last consideration: it may be that the authority of the supervisory and complaint machinery will not grow if Third World countries are increasingly pronounced guilty by a conciliation commission largely serving Western values—both normative and political.

TYPICAL SITUATIONS AND HUMAN RIGHTS CONVICTIONS

Hypothesis 10. Over time, convictions dealing with general human rights will increase most dramatically in frequency; convictions dealing with Cold War and decolonization issues will decline; convictions dealing with specific trade union issues will remain the same.

This hypothesis seems to be confirmed if we compare the data in Table 6 with those in Table 10. The convictions on human rights issues directed against authoritarian, mobilization, and modernizing autocratic regimes have been heaviest in recent years; the convictions on decolonization cases directed against economically growing and developed reconciliation regimes were heaviest in the mid-1950s, as were the Cold War convictions directed against mobilization regimes.

Of the 117 convictions (of which only 110 are tabulated) 63 per cent concerned human rights issues, 18 per cent Cold War issues, 12 per cent trade union issues, and 7 per cent decolonization issues. Though a total of 55 defendants appeared (48 are tabulated), they represent only 45 countries, the discrepancy resulting from changes in regime or institutions during the period covered.

It is hardly surprising that on the whole the authoritarian, oligarchical, and modernizing autocratic regimes have a worse record on human rights issues than they do on other issues. Nor is it surprising that the reconciliation regimes have better records, or that the majority of the mobilization regimes were convicted in the Cold War context. What *is* impressive is the overall impact of human rights issues, which increasingly overshadow all other issue contexts. By and large, the impact of trade union issues is minimal; only in the case of reconciliation regimes with capitalist institutions and underdeveloped economies can we note an unusually heavy number of true labor disputes, suggesting that in these countries conditions for practical approaches to the solution of labor conflict exist already or are developing rapidly.

In general, then, we have confirmed the hypothesis claiming an increasing incidence of human rights convictions against defendants other than Western-type reconciliation polities and socialist mobilization systems. However, the special importance of the human rights issues in our argument about value sharing compels a more detailed analysis. We have to know *what kinds of conditions*

TABLE 10

Freedom of Association: Defendant Types and Distribution of
Convictions by Issue, 1950–68

(*rank-ordered in terms of deviation from mean for human rights conviction, 63.2 per cent*)

Defendant type	Number of convictions	Number of defendants convicted[a]	Convictions				Deviation from mean	
			Cold war	Decolonization	Human rights	Trade union	Human rights	Trade union
Authoritarian Mixed Underdeveloped	8	3	0%	0%	100%	0%	+37	−12
Authoritarian Corporatist Underdeveloped	2	2	0	0	100	0	+37	−12
Modernizing oligarchy Capitalist Underdeveloped	2	2	0	0	100	0	+37	−12
Modernizing autocracy Capitalist Underdeveloped	2	2	0	0	100	0	+37	−12
Authoritarian Capitalist Underdeveloped	11	8	9	0	91	0	+27	−12
Not classifiable Capitalist Growing	8	1	0	0	88	13	+24	+1
Reconciliation Mixed Underdeveloped	10	6	0	0	80	20	+23	+8
Traditional oligarchy Capitalist Underdeveloped	6	3	0	0	83	17	+20	+5
Reconciliation Mixed Growing	9	3	0	33	56	11	−8	−1
Reconciliation Capitalist Underdeveloped	22	7	23	0	55	23	−9	+11
Authoritarian Mixed Growing	4	1	0	0	50	50	−13	+38
Reconciliation Mixed Developed	12	2	17	42	33	8	−30	−4
Mobilization Mixed Underdeveloped	3	2	67	0	33	0	−30	−12

TABLE 10 (*continued*)

Freedom of Association: Defendant Types and Distribution of Convictions by Issue, 1950–68

(*rank-ordered in terms of deviation from mean for human rights conviction, 63.2 per cent*)

Defendant type	Number of con- victions	Number of defen- dants con- victed[a]	Convictions				Deviation from mean	
			Cold war	Decoloni- zation	Human rights	Trade union	Human rights	Trade union
Mobilization Socialist Underdeveloped	3	2	67%	0%	33%	0%	−30	−12
Mobilization Socialist Growing	8	4	100	0	0	0	−63	−12

[a] Types accounting for less than 1 per cent of complaints were omitted. Identity of convicted defendants is the same as in Table 9. Excluded defendants identical with exclusions on Table 9.

produce violations that are singled out for condemnation. And we have to know especially what kinds of regimes are susceptible to these conditions and the consequences of those conditions. All this requires a closer look at the cases themselves.

Before we examine some of the typical situations that occur in the context of human rights convictions, a word is in order about the Cold War and decolonization issues that cluster around the lower half of Table 10. The 23 per cent figure for Cold War convictions against reconciliation regimes with capitalist institutions is largely accounted for by a number of complaints against Greece. These were brought by unions eager to be rid of the formidable legal restrictions imposed on all unions and union leaders suspected of sympathizing with the communists during the Greek civil war. Other cases in this category, under similar conditions, were brought in Chile.[1] All eight of the cases against mobilization-socialist-growing defendants involved global attacks by Western trade unions against a fundamental socialist practice: the use of trade unions as an arm of the ruling party to achieve basic economic objectives. Since freedom of association is, by definition, impossible in such a setting, the charges were brought not so much for obtaining an improvement in conditions as for scoring propaganda points.[2] It should be added that in four of these cases publicity sanctions accompanied the request to change law and practice. The only conviction of a developed reconciliation regime on Cold War charges was made in connection with Singapore, when Britain was condemned for her repressive measures against unions considered to be communist-infiltrated, measures continued, it should be noted, after the British withdrawal by the newly independent government of Singapore.[3]

Convictions on decolonization issues were handed out exclusively to France and Britain. Some of the most publicized cases involved the long, complex, and futile effort of the ILO to persuade France to exempt trade unions from the political repression practiced during the Algerian war.[4] Britain was asked to desist from suppressing trade unions, after she imposed restraints in many places during the 1950s in an effort to contain and limit the national movements there. Admittedly, it often proved impossible to distinguish between a national political party and its affiliated union militants. Yet repressive measures by the authorities as well as terrorism on the part of the nationalists did not respect the distinction between trade union and political status.[5]

This leaves us with human rights cases free from involvement in the broad political context. Seventy such convictions were handed down. They fall into three general categories. First and most frequent are cases in which a complainant sought to weaken or even topple an established and powerful repressive regime that controlled all trade unions or prohibited them. Second and almost as frequent are cases against regimes that attempted, sporadically and apparently without a deep commitment to an ideology or policy, to hamper and repress specific unions, without necessarily seeking to eliminate free trade unionism as an institution. Last and least common are cases against regimes that sought to eliminate hitherto free unions by absorbing them and subordinating them to a rigid national ideology and institutional structure, usually in the framework of a single-party state. We shall illustrate each of these situations.

Prominent among the governments committed on principle to preventing the growth of autonomous trade unions, and censured for that stand by the ILO, are South Africa, Spain, Portugal, Burundi, Liberia, Ghana (under Nkrumah), Thailand, Libya, Paraguay, Greece, and Britain (with respect to Southern Rhodesia); together they account for 31 adverse decisions. In South Africa, of course, the issue was and remains the package of laws and practices designed to prevent and control freedom of association for Africans in connection with the policy of *apartheid*.[6] Britain's inability to prevent the autonomous government of Southern Rhodesia (before 1965) from following a similar policy resulted in the only three convictions of this type scored against Western reconciliation regimes.[7] In a case against Portugal, the very principle of the subordination of unions to the corporate-authoritarian state was challenged, as it was in the early cases against Spain.[8] Later complaints against Spain also challenged the continued, though somewhat more relaxed, control over the Spanish workers, then seeking to reorganize and strike after 20 years of strict repression.[9] Complaints against Burundi, a traditional oligarchy, alleged that trade unionists had been murdered as part of a general policy of repression; a similar charge was brought against another traditional oligarchy, Paraguay, which has strictly controlled trade unionism for a long time.[10] Thailand and Libya, both modernizing autocracies in the period studied, had never permitted uncontrolled trade unionism and were censured for their actions.[11] So was authoritarian Liberia.[12] Nor did the repressive trade union practices of Nkrumah's Ghana, a mobilization regime that failed, go unchallenged.[13]

Our final exhibit in this category is unique in that it involves a reconciliation regime, albeit underdeveloped and with capitalist institutions. Feeling insecure after a long civil war with communist insurgents, Greece sought to strictly regulate trade unionism, registering unions, screening union leaders, controlling union funds and elections, and dissolving "undesirable" unions in an effort to keep communists out of the trade union movement. In doing so, she was convicted of infractions of freedom of association (after the Cold War was no longer a real threat) no fewer than eight times.[14]

Another 12 cases illustrate the opposite situation: efforts to bring a free trade union movement under tight state control and central direction. The measures complained against are uniformly similar: dissolution of dissident federations, police repression of meetings of workers attempting to keep their unions alive, arrest and imprisonment of uncooperative union leaders, refusal to permit unions to affiliate with Internationals, installation of government appointees to control sanctioned federations. Not surprisingly, the bulk of these infractions occur under authoritarian regimes in underdeveloped countries, usually in those with capitalist institutions but occasionally in those with mixed or even socialist institutions. But whatever the type, the purpose of the regime is invariably the containment of dissident elements in order to make possible the stable evolution of the country under single-party leadership.[15]

Finally, we must account for the other 27 convictions, those involving cases in which complainants sought protection against sporadic, if limited, efforts on the part of insecure democratic, oligarchical, and authoritarian regimes to control individual unions. The democratic cases are revealing. Costa Rica was censured for interfering with the efforts of plantation workers to organize themselves.[16] Brazil was found guilty, in the aftermath of the second Vargas regime, of limiting the freedom of association of public employees.[17] Japan proved vulnerable on the same score when, after regaining full independence, she tried to limit the right to strike and attempted to dismiss the leaders of certain civil service unions from their jobs.[18] In 1956 Chile was asked to amend its Law for the Permanent Defense of Democracy so as to avoid discriminating against unions, notably communist unions.[19] She was also censured for making it impossible for agricultural workers to organize themselves.[20] Pakistan was requested to reexamine its Public Security Law, which tended to repress trade unions as well as political groups.[21] Britain, in a case involving the Caribbean area, was warned against undue discrimination in the registration of unions.[22] Argentina was convicted four times under a democratic government and twice under an authoritarian one for essentially the same offenses: the discriminatory registration of unions and the withdrawal of registrations, the prohibition of certain strikes, the arrest and imprisonment of union leaders violating strike prohibitions, and the placing of unions of public employees under military administration.[23] The almost permanent divisions in Argentine society and the Argentine labor movement, between Peronist and revolutionary groups on one side and bourgeois-reformist elements on the other, are perfectly mirrored in the flood of Argentine cases, as is the recurring tendency of the military to intervene and place both groups under controls. Under the circumstances, the vagueness and self-contradictory nature of Argentine labor law hardly helps to clear up the situation.

In the authoritarian cases, the sporadic efforts at control show up equally clearly as evidence of regime insecurity. A Turkish conviction followed the refusal of the Menderes government to permit unions to affiliate with Internationals.[24] Jordan was asked not to dissolve "undesirable" unions arbitrarily.[25] Venezuela, under Pérez Jiménez, was sharply censured for brutally suppressing oil workers.[26] The military government of Honduras has been censured four times for rigging union elections, preventing elected union officers from taking office, denying registration to unions, and having strikers fired.[27]

SUMMARY

Our seven hypotheses about the characteristics of complainants, complaints, defendants, and convictions have stood up well. National trade unions have been progressively socialized into using the international protection machinery. Democratic trade unions are most successful in securing convictions of opponents. Complaints dealing with the general implications for political freedom implicit in union freedom of association have grown at the expense of propaganda charges, whereas violations of more limited trade union rights are the special preoccupation of unions in unstable and economically underdeveloped reconciliation polities with capitalist institutions.

With respect to the defendant countries, emphasis has shifted from the large powers and their global political confrontations to authoritarian and oligarchical regimes in Africa, Latin America, and—to a much lesser extent—Asia. As expected, oligarchical and authoritarian regimes have indeed been increasingly charged with violations of freedom of association in the larger context of social reform and democratization of institutions. On the other hand, contrary to our expectation, reconciliation polities with developed economies have not appeared more and more frequently as victims of complaints on trade union issues. As for convictions, the most common culprits turn out to be mobilization and authoritarian regimes, with human rights a central issue. Unstable democratic and oligarchical regimes, however, are almost as prominent, particularly those with capitalist institutions and underdeveloped economies.

Still, it is well to keep in mind that we probably cannot fully explore the possibilities of global value sharing unless we consider also the situations in which infractions arise. Our discussion of implementation will have to show which situations are most likely to be resolved through international action, thereby affording some clues about the future of a universal value system. One must consider, after all, that there may be a world of difference between an episodic violation linked to the vague fears of an unideological authoritarian or oligarchical regime, subject to learning and economic growth, and the deliberate stifling of domestic dissent in line with a specific development doctrine.

5. *Implementation*

Before a full assessment of the ILO experience can be made, a number of additional questions crucial for testing the functionalist strategy in the human rights context must be posed and answered. Functionalist theory assumes that as complainants and defendants increasingly use the international machinery, they will defer more and more to its authority; and suggests further that the supervisory machinery will gain in prestige and authority as its officials gather courage and address ever more severe and critical decisions to perennial defendants. One sign of the growing scope of the ILO committee's authority would be a willingness on the part of the members to widen the concept of freedom of association for trade unions so as to include related aspects of civil and political liberties. Such a step would be optimal for a gradual extension of human rights, for values to spread from an initial base commanding a cohesive client group and a reasonably well-defined consensus to an ever more controversial—but more important—area, with an even wider constituency among voluntary groups. The major question is: as the characteristics of the international system change, is a positive trend typical of one period carried over into the next? The answer must be "yes," if the functional strategy is to work. We then ask: Are adverse decisions more and more often carried out by defendants as the international system changes? Do the kinds of regimes that most need to improve their treatment of their citizens respond favorably to the ILO? In this connection, the functional strategy requires not only that decisions be carried out by defendants but that decisions dealing quite specifically with human rights cases be implemented.

THE LEGITIMACY OF THE ILO MACHINERY

The behavior of the ILO committee itself is our initial concern. The two propositions that require confirmation are:

Hypothesis 11a. Over time, the decisions of the ILO will become increasingly critical and severe with respect to the practices of defendant nations.

Hypothesis 11b. Over time, the decisions of the ILO will show more concern with general human rights and less with specific trade union grievances.

The simplest way of verifying Hypothesis 11a is to examine the type of decisions the committee has made over its 18-year history. They are recapitulated in Table 11. Quite clearly, decisions have *not* become more severe. Changes in law or practice were recommended in 21 per cent of the cases in the period after 1961; in the preceding tripolar period the rate was 33 per cent, even though the number of complaints was proportionately less. Furthermore, there has been a consistent decline in the number of dismissals with a recommendation to examine laws or practices. Finally, the frequency of sanctions has declined from a high of almost 5 per cent during the bipolar era to the recent low of 2.3 per cent. Clearly, the committee, appreciating the tenuous and even self-defeating character of this method of forcing compliance, has become much more reluctant to use it.

On the other hand, pre-decision inquiries have become more searching. In 1951 the committee dismissed 39 per cent of the complaints received without any kind of inquiry; in the most recent period that rate shrank to 23 per cent, while dismissals after inquiry rose to 38 per cent. In short, though the committee is not convicting nations more often (and though it continues to dismiss *sine die* complaints that are clearly trivial), it has become much more thorough in its procedure, making careful inquiries of the defendant government almost a matter of routine.

TABLE 11

Freedom of Association: Changes in Type of Decisions, 1950–68

Period	Number of cases	Decisions					
		Dismiss	Dismiss after inquiry	Dismiss with recommen- dation	Change law or practice	Sanc- tions	Pend- ing
1950–51	41	39%	34%	7%	15%	5%	0%
1952–55	88	32	34	17	14	2	1
1956–60	91	25	26	13	33	3	0
1961–68	266	23	38	10	21	2	6
Total	486	26%	35%	11%	21%	3%	4%

A more searching way of seeking validation of the hypothesis of increasing committee authority is to inquire when and under what circumstances the committee dismisses complaints, and whether the grounds for dismissal have shown some evolution over time. In the case of dismissals on grounds of insufficient evidence, the rate has declined from 50 per cent of all dismissals in 1951 to 34 per cent in the most recent period. But it is not clear whether this decline merely reflects greater care in preparation on the part of complainants as the procedure is better understood by client groups, or whether it is also the result of more extensive and prob- ing inquiry on the part of the ILO, which may develop new evi- dence through a correspondence with defendants or from the oral testimony they occasionally give. Complaints dismissed because the complaining party is not considered a *bona fide* client have been stabilized at 30 per cent for over ten years. The only visible evolution toward a relaxation of the stringent rules that determine which worker and employer groups have a *locus standi* before the committee has been in the admission of peasant unions, associa- tions of supervisory employees, and organizations of higher civil servants. Employer associations have been eligible all along, though only two or three exiled groups have taken advantage of their right to use ILO machinery.

Another ground for dismissal is the elapse of too much time between the filing of a complaint and the alleged illegal act. In such cases, the evidence may be murky, the defendant government may have changed, the complaining group may have been dissolved, the illegal act may have been remedied, or the committee may have simply come to the sad conclusion that because of local circumstances no purpose would be served by continuing the investigation. Dismissals on these grounds have risen from 15.6 per cent in 1951 to almost 27 per cent in the most recent period, suggesting the ILO's growing realization that its supervisory machinery continues to be hampered by strong national resistance.

But of all the indicators of growing scope, the most sensitive is the evolution of the committee's rule that only trade union issues merit a hearing. Here the ILO's definition is not the same as ours: for the ILO a trade union issue is a violation of Convention 87 or Convention 98 that (1) is *not* an intrinsic part of a general political situation involving civil war, riots, or sedition, and (2) is *not* an economic demand for increases in worker benefits. Thus, in principle the ILO will dismiss as "not a trade union issue" cases of alleged violations of freedom of association in the context of governmental control of sedition and treason or in the context of a breakdown in collective bargaining on substantive issues. But these self-imposed limits on jurisdiction are far from self-evident when applied to concrete situations. A widening of scope would clearly be implicit in a willingness to stretch the meaning of a "trade union issue." The record shows that the rate of dismissal on these grounds declined steadily, from a high of 34.4 per cent in 1951 to a low of about 9 per cent during the last ten years! It is through this interpretive technique that the committee has shifted the focus of its work, a shift that is reflected in the growing number of human rights cases coded in our classification scheme.

This evolution is detectable also in the jurisprudence of the committee. One watershed was reached around 1958, when two doctrines that had operated in favor of state dominance over voluntary groups were gradually cut down by the committee. One was the distinction between "political" concerns and "trade union" issues; the other was the ruling, confirmed a number of times, that certain countries in the early stages of economic development could properly regulate key trade union activities, such as elections, finances, and the conduct of officers,[1] could insist on the separation of political and trade union activities, and could subject unions to government registration. These two doctrines, which clearly overlap, operated in favor of the colonial powers before the flood of decolonization in Africa and Asia. And they legitimated a wide range of governmental controls aimed at purging communists from union leadership. Thus special screening and security measures were considered legal, and the conviction of union leaders on allegations of sedition were considered criminal offenses not protected by Conventions 87 and 98. Prior to 1958, the ILO Committee upheld practices of this kind in Chile, Switzerland, South Africa, the United States, the Netherlands, Malaya, India, Greece, and Britain.

The evolution away from the restriction of trade union activity in the colonial context is illustrated in several cases. For example, France was acquitted for interfering with Tunisian unions, and then was slightly restrained from similar efforts in Morocco; but a case involving Algeria brought about a different approach and a much wider view of the permissible field of action of trade unions in developing nations.[2] The same trend appears in a number of cases against Britain.[3] Complaints of union repression in the context of anti-communist and anti-liberationist campaigns were dismissed by the committee under the "early development" and "not a trade union issue" doctrines until the mid-1950s.[*] It remains to be seen what the jurisprudence of the committee will be as equally militant movements of this kind spring up in the newly independent countries of Africa and in the older nations of Latin America now seething with social unrest.

The cases against Greece, Spain, and South Africa are also instructive. The ILO continued to close its eyes to most of the anti-

* The break came with Case 136 (U.K.–Cyprus, 1955–59) ; in the first phase the committee continued to brook the concentration camp method of containment used by Britain in the Cyprus hostilities of the early 1950s, but in the second phase this was held no longer admissible, even though the factual and legal context had not changed. In Case 103 (U.K.–Southern Rhodesia, 1954), a more extensive policy against racial discrimination was also expressed.

union practices of the Greek government long after the end of the civil war, and excused the many restrictions on grounds of defense against sedition. Not until 1958 did the committee deny the Greek argument that a state of national emergency still existed.[4] At first, the committee felt that racial discrimination *per se* did not violate Convention 87 or Convention 98; but by 1954 it decided that the imposition of a racial criterion in determining the right to organize was a restraint on freedom of association, even if that racial criterion was applied to the entire society and not just to unions.[5] In this connection, it should be noted the ILO continues to accept Portugal's arguments that trade union repression is justified since it is part of a general policy aimed at containing communist sedition.[6]

What, then, is the picture with respect to the scope of the right of freedom of association insofar as more recent cases in the Third World are concerned? Practice is by no means uniform; the trend seemingly inaugurated with the wider interpretation applied to the former colonial powers, and Greece, South Africa, and Spain, is not consistently carried over into the tangled trade union and political situation in Africa and Latin America. For instance, the committee reaffirmed that a government has the right to regulate trade unions and trade unionists whenever their activities conflict with general legislation dealing with subversion and sedition, or fall afoul of rules governing public order—particularly when, as in the cases under scrutiny, the union activities had been part of a general political struggle against authoritarian regimes.[7] In dismissing a complaint against the Congo Brazzaville government, the committee declared:

The fundamental and permanent mission of the trade union movement is the economic and social advancement of the workers. . . . When trade unions in accordance with national law and practice of their respective countries and at the decision of their members decide to establish relations with a political party or to undertake political action as a means toward advancement of their economic and social objectives, such political relations or actions should not be of such a nature as to compromise the continuance of the trade union movement or its social or economic functions irrespective of political changes in the country.[8]

However, in a later case against the same country, the committee reversed itself, finding that a violation of Convention 87 had taken place under circumstances not fundamentally different from those that led to the earlier exoneration.[9] Furthermore, similar situations in Ecuador, Burundi, and the Dominican Republic were censured in strong terms, even though conditions of domestic unrest had certainly existed at the time the illegal acts were committed.[10] Finally, we should note that when a government is pitted against a union and the committee is confronted with a directly contradictory set of statements and allegations, the government will invariably prevail, even in disputes involving the most mundane trade union matters, such as the right to housing, discriminatory promotion practices, and grievance procedures.[11]

We conclude, therefore, that Hypothesis 11a is refuted and Hypothesis 11b is confirmed: decisions of the committee have not become more severe, but the scope of the right to freedom of association has been slowly enlarged by interpretation, even though the committee has not exercised a freer interpretation uniformly among the member nations.

The legitimacy of the committee has clearly improved. One evidence of this is the doubling in the number of complaints between the last period and the preceding one (see Table 6). Only the East European socialist nations continue to dispute the practice of hailing accused governments before the bar of the ILO; but they question the representative character of the committee rather than the legal principles on which it is based. Even South Africa, before her withdrawal from the ILO, cooperated with the procedure to the extent of answering inquiries and furnishing explanations of her policy. The earliest targets of sanctions — Peru, Venezuela, Hungary, Poland, Czechoslovakia, and the Soviet Union — refused to admit the Fact-Finding and Conciliation Commission when that procedure was first invoked, and denied any obligation to submit to international jurisdiction. Now, however, countries singled out for severe criticism have been known to invite the commission or other ILO missions to visit them in an effort to justify their actions. Among the nations that have done so are Costa Rica,

Libya, Burundi, Japan, Greece, and Spain.[12] It must be added that the sanctions in the Cold War cases were imposed in a spirit of ideological crusading, whereas the committee more recently has stressed conciliation and compromise, careful fact-finding, and the hearing and cross-examination of witnesses, and has attempted to do justice to the local circumstances giving rise to infringements of union freedom. And if the committee has been inconsistent in its interpretation of trade union issues, it has nevertheless remained steadfast in its refusal to accept as final and determinative a *government's claim* that a given complaint is purely political, reserving such a finding for itself. As for those who have remained unconvinced of the committee's impartiality, the Governing Body, recognizing the problem, has sought to shore up the committee's legitimacy by amending the Standing Orders: members must now disqualify themselves if their countries are parties in a case, or if, as international union officials, they had a personal hand in drawing up a complaint.[13]

THE IMPLEMENTATION OF ADVERSE DECISIONS

Hypothesis 12. Over time, a growing number of defendants will implement adverse decisions.

Table 12 gives no comfort on this score. In only 11 per cent of the convictions handed out were the decisions fully implemented; put more brutally, this means that of 117 adverse decisions, only 13 resulted in complete remedial action by the defendant government! Moreover, the rate of full compliance has declined appreciably in the most recent period. It is true that the rate of complete "no improvement" performances also declined slightly; but it has risen again during the most recent, and most active, period. Almost 60 per cent of all adverse decisions remain unexecuted!

Looking at the same figures from another perspective, we note the astonishing fact that the combined rate of "great" and "some" improvement has remained virtually stable since the inception of the ILO machinery in 1951, when a 38 per cent level was achieved; after dropping to a low of 35 per cent, the rate has risen to 40 per cent in the latest period. In short, the gross figures suggest indiffer-

TABLE 12

Freedom of Association: Implementation of Adverse Decisions, 1950–68

Period	Number of cases	Implementation of adverse decisions		
		Great improvement	Some improvement	No improvement
1950–51	8	13%	25%	62%
1952–55	14	21	14	65
1956–60	33	18	30	52
1961–68	62	5	35	60
Total	117	11%	31%	58%

ent performance as concerns implementation. Implementation did not improve markedly over time. This finding fully accords with the poor implementation record we discovered when we examined Hypothesis 1 in the context of the work of the Committee of Experts on the Application of Conventions.

Unfortunately, we can draw very few inferences for value sharing from these data. Even in the instance of full compliance, years of correspondence and numerous warnings and admonitions are often required before remedial action is taken. The same is true of the partial compliances. Moreover, our coding of "some improvement" does not necessarily mean that the most serious and far-reaching of several infractions in a case was remedied. Very frequently, for instance, a defendant discontinued a specific practice while leaving the law permitting the practice unchanged.

At this point the limitations of our data dictate caution. One could argue that an implementation rate between 35 and 40 per cent over almost two decades suggests a definite sharing of values. But the uneven and inconsistent nature of *what* is being implemented makes it unwise to jump to such a conclusion. Suppose that Latin American countries gradually cease the practice of discriminatory compulsory registration of unions, and that African countries persist in the practice but permit their unions to reaffiliate with Internationals. Would such a pattern of implementation suggest a progressive and global sharing of important values? Would progress toward the *de facto* recogniton of autonomous unions in

Argentina, not matched by similar developments in Argentine law, constitute evidence of progressive value sharing? In short, all we can say with assurance is that implementation has not improved with international systems change. But neither has it deteriorated. As to whether this augurs well or ill for the sharing of values, we cannot pretend to be categorical.

As we saw when he examined Hypothesis 2, when it comes to the question of strengthening the authority of international norms, nations differ in performance according to the degree of economic development and the type of regime. Hence we suggest:

Hypothesis 13. Adverse decisions are always most readily implemented by reconciliation and insecure authoritarian and oligarchical regimes; stable authoritarian and oligarchical regimes gradually implement more adverse decisions; mobilization regimes almost never implement adverse decisions.

Table 13 gives little support to these notions. True, mobilization regimes perform as poorly as predicted, this despite the fact that many of their convictions were accompanied by sanctions. South Africa, of course, proved just as unresponsive; after her withdrawal from the ILO, a committee of experts was appointed in 1967 by ECOSOC to look into charges of trade union infringements, thus continuing the futile work of the ILO committee.[14] The performance of traditional and modernizing oligarchies is also indifferent; so is the performance of authoritarian regimes in underdeveloped countries with capitalist institutions. Authoritarian regimes in countries with mixed institutions perform fairly well, as do some reconciliation clusters. But honesty forces us to note that there are clusters of reconciliation regimes with relatively poor records. All in all, the truth seems to be a good deal more complex than Hypothesis 13 would suggest.

Nor does international systems change help us in approximating our hypothesis. Table 14 breaks down the implementation data by periods. Though economically developed reconciliation regimes improved their performance, it is clear that even after the decline in decolonization cases, economically underdeveloped and growing reconciliation regimes did not; in short, no uniform finding for democratic nations can be uncovered. Authoritarian regimes with

TABLE 13
Freedom of Association: Defendant Types and Implementation of Adverse Decisions

Defendant type	Number of convictions	Implementation of adverse decisions		
		Great improvement	Some improvement	No improvement
Reconciliation Mixed Developed	12	33%	42%	25%
Authoritarian Mixed Underdeveloped	8	0	75	25
Reconciliation Mixed Underdeveloped	10	40	20	40
All other authoritarian	7	0	57	43
Reconciliation Mixed Growing	8	13	38	50
Reconciliation Capitalist Underdeveloped	22	14	27	59
All modernizing oligarchies	5	20	20	60
Traditional oligarchy Capitalist Underdeveloped	6	0	33	67
Authoritarian Capitalist Underdeveloped	11	0	27	73
All other mobilization	8	0	13	88
Mobilization Socialist Growing	8	0	0	100
Not classifiable Capitalist Growing	8	0	0	100
Mean for all adverse decisions	117	11	31	58

TABLE 14

Freedom of Association: Implementation of Adverse Decisions and Defendant Types, 1950–68

Defendant type	Period	Number of convicted countries	Number of convictions	Great improvement —%	Some improvement —%	No improvement —%	Mean nonimplementation score
Authoritarian	1950–51	0	0	—	—	—	
Mixed	1952–55	0	0	—	—	—	
Underdeveloped	1956–60	1	1	0	100	0	
	1961–68	3	7	0	71	29	25
Reconciliation	1950–51	0	0	—	—	—	
Mixed	1952–55	1	2	50	0	50	
Developed	1956–60	2	3	67	33	0	
	1961–68	1	7	14	57	29	25
Reconciliation	1950–51	1	1	0	0	100	
Mixed	1952–55	1	1	100	0	0	
Underdeveloped	1956–60	2	3	67	33	0	
	1961–68	3	5	20	20	60	40
All other	1950–51	0	0	—	—	—	
Authoritarian	1952–55	0	0	—	—	—	
	1956–60	1	1	0	100	0	
	1961–68	2	2	0	50	50	33
Reconciliation	1950–51	1	1	100	0	0	
Mixed	1952–55	1	1	0	0	100	
Growing	1956–60	2	6	0	50	50	
	1961–68	0	0	—	—	—	50
Authoritarian	1950–51	0	0	—	—	—	
Mixed	1952–55	0	0	—	—	—	
Growing	1956–60	0	0	—	—	—	
	1961–68	1	4	0	50	50	50

				0%	0%	100%	
All modernizing oligarchies & modernizing autocracies	1950–51	1	1	0	0	100%	57
	1952–55	1	1	0	0	100	
	1956–60	4	4	25	50	25	
	1961–68	1	1	0	0	100	
Reconciliation	1950–51	1	1	0	100	0	59
Capitalist	1952–55	2	4	25	50	25	
Underdeveloped	1956–60	3	5	20	0	80	
	1961–68	4	12	8	25	67	
Traditional	1950–51	0	0	—	—	—	67
oligarchy	1952–55	0	0	—	—	—	
Capitalist	1956–60	1	1	0	100	0	
Underdeveloped	1961–68	3	5	0	20	80	
Authoritarian	1950–51	0	0	—	—	—	73
Capitalist	1952–55	0	0	—	—	—	
Underdeveloped	1956–60	2	2	0	0	100	
	1961–68	7	9	0	33	67	
All other	1950–51	1	1	0	0	100	88
Mobilization	1952–55	2	2	0	0	100	
	1956–60	0	0	—	—	—	
	1961–68	4	5	0	20	80	
Mobilization	1950–51	2	2	0	0	100	100
Socialist	1952–55	2	2	0	0	100	
Growing	1956–60	3	4	0	0	100	
	1961–68	0	0	—	—	—	
Not classifiable	1950–51	0	0	—	—	—	100
Capitalist	1952–55	1	1	0	0	100	
Growing	1956–60	1	3	0	0	100	
	1961–68	1	4	0	0	100	

TABLE 15

Most Frequently Cited Defendants, Implementation of Adverse Decisions, and Human Rights Scores, 1950–68

Country[a]	Number of complaints	Number of convictions	Number of unimplemented decisions	Percentage of default	Human rights score[b] (Rowe Scale)	
					All issues	Less politicized issues
United Kingdom	48	11	3	27%	−.29	−.09
Greece	45	14	10	71	.23	.30
France	26	3	2	67	−.26	.08
Argentina	24	10	5	50	.35	.40
South Africa	19	8	8	100	−.57	−.23
Morocco	15	0	–	–	.65	.14
Congo (Kinshasa)	14	0	–	–	.81	.32
United States	14	0	–	–	.00	.02
Spain	13	7	1	14	.05	.26
India	11	0	–	–	.59	.24
Chile	10	4	0	0	.60	.49
Colombia	10	2	2	100	.38	.38
Dominican Rep.	10	1	1	100	.29	.42
Peru	10	2	0	0	.36	.33
Honduras	10	4	2	50	.51	.30
Costa Rica	8	3	2	67	.42	.37
Cuba	8	3	3	100	.53	.21
Brazil	7	3	0	0	.33	.39
Ecuador	7	3	2	67	.55	.47
Guatemala	7	3	3	100	.58	.41
Venezuela	6	2	2	100	.47	.39
Japan	5	2	0	0	.26	.12
Hungary	4	3	3	100	.58	.08
Poland	2	2	2	100	.53	.12
Soviet Union	2	2	2	100	.52	.08

[a] All defendants with ten or more complaints and/or two convictions against them included.

[b] Human rights scores for 1946–66. For an explanation of the Rowe Scale, see p. 18 above. The score here reported is the 20-year average. Less politicized issues include human rights resolutions other than those dealing with South Africa, the Cold War, and the decolonization struggle.

capitalist institutions have gradually become more responsive as authoritarian regimes with mixed institutions have grown less so. Only mobilization systems (with one exception in Africa) appear to go their consistently unresponsive way.

How do the most frequently convicted nations respond to the publicity to which the machinery exposes them? Does this way of looking at the record suggest an interpretation more satisfactory than Hypothesis 13? A comparison of several countries with the same attributes, as presented in Table 15, reveals that, apart from mobilization regimes and developed reconciliation polities, we cannot make any prediction at all on the basis of our defendant typology. Japan, Chile, and Peru are responsive; Greece, Costa Rica, and Colombia are not. Democratic Brazil (and to some extent even the Brazilian military regime) heeds the ILO; democratic Argentina does so only part of the time. Authoritarian Spain proves to be very responsive to the authority of the ILO; authoritarian Guatemala, Honduras, and Cuba flout it.

Hypothesis 14. Adverse decisions are most commonly implemented by defendant nations when prosecuted jointly or simultaneously by several trade union Internationals.

The short answer is "not so." Jointly presented complaints resulting in convictions received full or partial implementation 48 per cent of the time, only slightly better than the mean implementation score of 42 per cent. But the ICFTU and the WFTU, separately, did just as well. National unions, on the other hand, score much more poorly. Progressive value sharing through joint action and muted intra-labor cleavages cannot be deduced from this pattern any more legitimately than from the national performances analyzed above.

A final question about implementation must be cleared up: which types of issues are most often acted upon? The answer is crucial to a functional strategy, for the functionalist pins his hope on human rights decisions being implemented more faithfully than other kinds of decisions, thus leading to a sharing of values on issues most vital to the development of a global consensus on personal liberties.

Hypothesis 15. Adverse decisions are implemented most frequently if the complaint arose in a functionally specific and narrow "trade union" context; they are implemented least frequently if the context is highly politicized through links with the Cold War and decolonization struggles.

Though this hypothesis does not claim a preferred status on implementation for human rights cases, these cases should certainly show more compliance than the politicized cases, and should not do much worse than trade union cases. Table 16 suggests that our hypothesis is in part correct. Cold War–connected decisions are indeed least likely to be complied with. And though trade union convictions are comparatively few in number, corrective action has been taken in well over half of the cases. But our hypothesis tends to break down with respect to our second category of politicization: adverse decisions rendered in the context of the decolonization struggle are taken very seriously indeed by the only defendant really concerned—Great Britain—which has taken action almost two-thirds of the time.

On the whole, the world's record in fully implementing human rights decisions—the most crucial for the purpose of establishing, widening, and standardizing fundamental values—is dismal. Even so, we must examine the implementation record and the type of issues involved more closely. The ILO procedure proved almost completely powerless to prevent the establishment of tight governmental controls over relatively free trade unions; in only two of the 12 cases in that category was there evidence of some responsive-

TABLE 16

Freedom of Association: Implementation and Issues, 1950–68

Issue	Number of convictions	Implementation of adverse decisions		
		Great improvement	Some improvement	No improvement
Cold war	21	0%	24%	76%
Decolonization	8	50	13	37
Human rights	74	7	35	59
Trade union	14	29	28	43
Total	117	11%	31%	58%

ness on the part of the accused governments. However, the picture is not quite as dismal when the issue was controls that had been in effect for some time. Thirty-one such cases occurred; in not one was great improvement forthcoming as a result of censure, but partial improvement was scored in 12 (five of them involving Spain). These findings suggest that a newly determined resolve to suppress freedom of association is not easily deterred, but that an established and possibly waning resolve stands some chance of being shaken by an international appeal. Finally, cases in our third category—repression that is not part of a deliberate and general policy—respond very well to ILO intervention. Of the 27 cases so coded, four showed great improvement and another 11 some improvement. This suggests that if any one category of offender is to provide the main impetus for international value sharing, it is likely to be this one.

SUMMARY

That the poor record on implementing adverse decisions undermines our earlier positive conclusions is painfully obvious. The indirect strategy of protecting human rights is hardly advanced when the complainants and the supervisory machinery meet the functional requisites—but the defendants do not.

Over time, ILO decisions have not become more severe or more critical. But they have become more careful and more searching, and in fact more closely approximate negotiation than peremptory judicial rulings. Moreover, ILO decisions *do* show more and more concern for general human rights and *do* reflect a deliberate attempt to broaden the scope of the rights to be protected. Meanwhile, defendants, as a group, have not improved their record in implementing adverse decisions; but neither does the record show that, overall, they have grown less cooperative. Nevertheless, the rate of full implementation of ILO rulings has declined sharply over the years, and the rate of partial implementation has improved only slightly. Once more, the international procedure has gained more legitimacy, but its authority remains very much in doubt. Adverse decisions are almost never carried out by mobilization regimes; but then, they are not very well executed by any other type of regime either. Though we find reconciliation regimes with mixed institutions and developed economies and authoritarian regimes with mixed institutions and underdeveloped economies more faithful to their obligations than others, there are large differences among countries within the same cluster. The fact is, one cannot predict submission to ILO authority by defendant attributes with consistency or reliability.

Two further points in summary: we must admit that the regimes most in need of supervision are the least responsive, whereas some of those least in need of it are the most responsive. Thus we can take little comfort from the finding that adverse decisions dealing with human rights pure and simple are somewhat better implemented than decisions arising in the context of the Cold War. Having said this, we must see in these findings the single most destructive piece of evidence against our neo-functional thesis of piecemeal and incremental sharing of important values. To appreciate the implications of this conclusion, we must turn again to the specific cases. Only they can help us pinpoint which type of defendant offers the best hope for better implementation in the future.

6. *The Effectiveness of the System*

C. Wilfred Jenks, noting the growing potency of world public opinion, as represented in ILO proceedings by the large Internationals, suggests that the machinery for protecting freedom of association has worked best when the principle of international accountability is used to persuade governments guilty of "an error of judgment in the application of national laws and regulations" to mend their ways. "In such cases," he says, "effective redress by national procedures may be, and in certain cases appears to have been, facilitated by the possibility of international enquiry."[1] He notes further that direct discussions between the ILO committee and a government acting in good faith have served as an effective method of conciliation; as a result governments and unions are able to work together amicably after a case has been settled. Finally, he points out that general recommendations issued by the committee in pursuance of a complaint have sometimes served as a viable program for industrial peace, accomplishing more in the end than might have been achieved by a formal condemnation.

This is certainly a telling and accurate appraisal. It recognizes that mobilization regimes are impervious to the pressure generated by the ILO machinery, since they are indifferent to that elusive world opinion to which optimists pin their hopes. (In fact, we are entitled to ask whether such opinion can be postulated as a *precondition* for the success of systems of protection, when our concern is to inquire how the system can *usher in* a consensus.) This appraisal also recognizes that reconciliation regimes have little need of international pressure, since the pressure of domestic opinion is usually sufficient for the protection of rights.

Jenks rightly leaves us with intermediate cases as the most important beneficiaries of the system. And yet, even here, he counsels caution in evaluating the record:

There must be patience. In these matters little is achieved quickly. This is of course a limitation of the value of the procedure as an effective protection against imminent and irrevocable wrong. The ILO procedures, which it has taken almost fifty years to bring to their present stage of development, have saved some men's lives and secured the release of others, promptly and less promptly, from prison or protective custody, but have been more effective, both in large matters of policy and in respect of particular persons or incidents, in securing the redress of mistakes and wrongs the nature of which permitted of second thoughts than in their initial prevention.[2]

But since these general remarks fail to tell us which of these intermediate cases are crucial, we must make our own effort to pinpoint them. The implementation record of the defendant governments is summarized in Table 17 in terms of regimes. It can help us give some weight to Jenks's general observations.

The eye jumps to the column "great improvement," where we note that 12 of the 13 instances of such performance were contrib-

TABLE 17

Freedom of Association: Regime Types and Implementation of Adverse Decisions, 1950–68

Regime type	Number of convictions	Number of implemented decisions			Number of unimplemented decisions	Default percentage
		Great	Some	Total		
Not classifiable	8	0	0	0	8	100%
Mobilization	14	0	1	1	13	93
Traditional oligarchy	6	0	2	2	4	67
Modernizing oligarchy	5	1	1	2	3	60
Authoritarian	32	0	14	14	18	56
Modernizing autocracy	2	0	1	1	1	50
Reconciliation (underdeveloped)	28	7	8	15	13	47
Reconciliation (growing, developed)	22	5	9	14	8	36
Total	117	13	36	49	68	

uted by reconciliation regimes. Sudan, then a modernizing oligarchy, was the one exception. Again, in the "some improvement" column, half of those tabulated are reconciliation regimes. But more interesting here is the question: which were the authoritarian regimes that showed responsiveness? The answer: Spain, Argentina, Honduras, Ghana, and Brazil. We might ask the same question in connection with modernizing and traditional oligarchies and modernizing autocracies. We established earlier that these regime types were indifferent performers; still it is important to know specifically which countries do respond. Our answer here is Thailand, Paraguay, Ecuador, and Jordan. And as a last question: if reconciliation regimes do not, as a rule, require the push of an international machinery, how do we account for 13 unimplemented decisions on the part of economically underdeveloped democracies? Greece accounts for the bulk of them, Costa Rica and Colombia for most of the rest.

THE CASES OF GREAT IMPROVEMENT

Of the 13 cases of great improvement, none occurred in the Cold War context; but four concerned matters of decolonization.[3] Hence they can teach us only that democratic countries, already under pressure at home and abroad to cut back overseas involvements, are willing to go along with human rights procedures in hastening their own demise as colonial powers. Few would argue that France proved responsive to nationalist unions in Morocco, and Britain to union militants in Cyprus, Northern Rhodesia, and eventually even Aden, primarily because of pressure from Geneva. In fact, implementation came automatically as these governments, for different reasons, decided to yield to nationalist pressure in those countries. International concern, at best, served as a shadowy midwife in their birth.

Trade union cases account for another four of our exhibits of great improvement. In one, international pressure and conciliation were able to unite with domestic opposition in staving off an amendment to the Uruguayan labor code that would have greatly strengthened the government's power to control unions.[4] In a second, the ILO, concomitantly with the election of a reconciliation regime in Peru, was able to persuade the incoming government to grant union organizing rights to public employees.[5] In the third, the ILO procedure allowed opponents to expose the discriminatory trade union registration and recognition regulations followed by the government of Newfoundland and brought about the enactment of a new set of rules.[6] And in the last, the ILO even commanded enough authority in Greece to resolve a dispute involving an official of the taxi drivers' union whose driver's license had been lifted and who was apparently being harassed by the police.[7]

We are thus left with only six genuine human rights cases. ILO successes in Japan, Brazil, and Chile are further examples of cases in which domestic opposition to existing legislation, the use to good advantage of a change in conditions, and the availability of an international forum to put pressure on the government all played a part.[8] All three instances, it must be stressed, reflect a situation in which legitimate domestic groups, opposing a democratic government, simply made use of the opportunity to appeal to an international forum for additional support in a campaign they might well have won anyway. In Brazil this meant that the incoming Kubitschek government put a stop to discriminatory practices against unions suspected of communist domination; in Chile it involved the repeal of the Act for the Permanent Defense of Democracy; in Japan it led to the present uneasy truce between the major public employees unions and the government.

Sudan provides a much more telling example, though one cannot be very sanguine about the chances of a permanent change. In 1958 the modernizing oligarchy under General Abboud suppressed all trade unions, stopped their newspapers, and arrested their leaders. The government did not respond to ILO remonstrances until 1960, when it explained that new procedures for registering trade unions were under consideration. Though the Sudanese authorities continued to be vague on the subject of freedom of the press and the fate of the arrested leaders, they assured the ILO in 1962 that many unions had been registered. But the ILO replied that the Trade Union Ordinance of 1960, under which the registrations were going forward, still vested far too much power in the registrar to be compatible with Convention 87. In 1964, after the successful revolt against the Abboud regime, Sudan confirmed that full freedom had been restored, and that the 1960 Ordinance had been repealed.[9]

THE CASES OF SOME IMPROVEMENT

Of the much more numerous instances of partial implementation, only a few involved genuine trade union issues. After the fall of Perón, Argentina cautiously and inconsistently eliminated some of her discriminatory practices in union registration, and temporarily suspended her prohibition of strikes by public employees. In mobilization-oriented Somalia, the same concession was made, and in Greece some union-proposed reforms in the composition of arbitration boards were introduced.[10]

More significant for our thesis is the incidence of Cold War–connected improvements. Here again we encounter the phenomenon of domestic opposition groups, in a putative democratic setting, allying themselves with the global machinery in pursuit of union objectives—the elimination of regulations allowing the government to screen suspected communists from union leadership. In Brazil, Chile, and Japan, during the height of the Korean War, some success was scored in that the governments of those countries retained the regulations but relaxed their rigorous application. Even in Greece some small concessions were made by the security-conscious government.[11]

The lessons of greatest importance must be culled from the human rights context proper. The most interesting cases turn out to be those involving authoritarian regimes with mixed economic institutions and on the way to economic growth, viz., Argentina, Ghana, Spain, and Brazil since 1964, which together account for eight of 27 cases in this category. In the reconciliation regime group, a few cases concerned Britain's not wholly successful attempts to eliminate racial discrimination in territories under her control; these cases have little meaning for us, since the territories involved have become self-governing.[12] More interesting are those in which less developed reconciliation regimes took halting steps toward implementation: Greece reversed the arbitrary dismissal of a few dissident union leaders; Costa Rica moderated the practice of intimidation of plantation workers on one occasion; Peru lifted her prohibitions against the union rights of public employees; Chile took some first steps toward permitting agricultural workers to organize; and Argentina, in her democratic interlude, restored freedom of the press to unions and relaxed (but did not repeal) the Industrial Association Act of 1958, which discriminated against Peronist unions.[13] Some of the economically underdeveloped authoritarian countries, but only a few, also took remedial action: Liberia slightly relaxed her restraints on plantation workers and her prohibitions against international affiliation of her unions; Turkey also relented on the question of affiliation; and Honduras registered some dissident unions and reinstated union leaders removed by the government.[14] Among traditional oligarchies, Paraguay and Ecuador moderated, but did not completely abandon, their policy of controlling union organizing efforts.[15] In 1958 Thailand, a modernizing autocracy, suppressed all trade unions and arrested most of the leaders. Over the next decade unions remained illegal, and despite repeated assurances from Bangkok to Geneva that a new labor code would soon be drafted, in the judgment of the ILO the document finally produced did not meet the terms of Convention 87; as of 1967 Thai responsiveness was limited to the release of the arrested leaders.[16]

In sum, the improvement in underdeveloped authoritarian nations, traditional oligarchies, and modernizing autocracies is so fragmentary, and is, moreover, subject to such easy reversal with the slightest movement in regime, that the process of international value sharing can hardly take solace from it. The most consistent pattern of partial implementation has been contributed by young reconciliation regimes with underdeveloped or growing economies and thus the hope for an intensification of the process must be founded on these nations, and on the activities of their trade unions in company with the Internationals.

One additional type of prospective client requires emphasis:

authoritarian nations in the process of evolution, with mixed or even socialist institutions and a strong rate of economic growth. Spain, the most important case, will be discussed below. Ghana also belongs in this category. The post-Nkrumah military regime went some way in meeting an ILO condemnation of political interference in trade union activity, which had taken these forms: the Convention People's Party control over the Trades Union Congress, curtailing the right to strike and the right to form other unions, as well as the government's arrest of dissident leaders.[17] In 1965 the new government enacted an Industrial Relations Law that remedied a few of these practices, though in the opinion of the ILO committee it still fell far short of the requirements of Convention 87. The military regime in Argentina followed the same inconsistent line, moderating some government controls and reasserting others that its democratic predecessor had followed. After 1964, Brazil's military junta systematically took over all unions and purged leaders deemed subversive. Once the purge had been completed, union elections were permitted in at least some unions, while others apparently continued to be subject to state intervention. Though the Brazilian military has, in general, refused to cooperate with the ILO committee, some responsiveness has been shown in the release of a number of arrested union leaders and in the imposition of a relatively light sentence on one prominent leader, whose fate was singled out by the ILO for searching questions.[18] In short, an insecure authoritarian regime that finds an articulate and reasonably well-developed trade union movement functioning when it assumes power, will occasionally bow to international criticism. Moreover, as the case of Spain shows, such a regime may even actively cooperate in its own transition when international and national forces pressing for change happen to converge.

THE MOST INSTRUCTIVE CASES: SPAIN, GREECE, AND JAPAN

We have concluded that the defendants most likely to implement adverse decisions relating to basic human rights are young reconciliation regimes and authoritarian polities with a history of active trade unionism, both national and international. Our three case studies of such nations involve some of the most celebrated complaints in the history of the ILO procedure. Each complaint—or series of related complaints—concerned a major piece of national legislation challenged by some force in the country; each saw one or more of the large Internationals giving support to, or seeking the adherence of, important national unions; each continued over at least a decade; and each resulted in the firing of the biggest gun in the ILO arsenal, a special on-the-spot inquiry, after repeated condemnations by the Committee on Freedom of Association.

The Case of Spain. The success of the ILO in Spain is, of course, closely connected with the internal pressure for reform that has existed in Spanish society, and even within the Spanish government, for over a decade. But pressure was exerted from another direction, too, notably when very old trade union organizations, operating in part clandestinely in Spain and in part in exile in other countries on the Continent, were able to obtain the ready support of the big Internationals in the fight for change. In 1956 the ICFTU and the General Union of Spanish Workers (in exile) presented a sweeping complaint, attacking the entire structure of corporatist *sindicatos* as incompatible with freedom of association and the right to bargain collectively; in addition, the government's repression of the attempted general strike of 1951 was specifically attacked. The ILO committee responded by requesting the Spanish government to amend its labor charter and penal code to meet the requirements of Conventions 87 and 98—no mean order, since what the ILO in fact asked was that a corporatist regime disestablish itself, not only with respect to the kind of voluntary organizations permitted but also with respect to the kind of negotiated agreements those organizations could conclude. In 1958 the complaint was amended when new allegations were submitted simultaneously by the WFTU and the ICFTU. In March of that year the government had attempted first to prohibit and then to repress a wave of strikes by miners and some industrial workers. The new attack therefore concentrated on the right to strike and on the persecution of trade union leaders, in this instance the leaders who had sought to take advantage of the labor unrest to reestablish unions dissolved in the aftermath of the civil war. The government's initial response, in 1960, was to empower the Minister of the Interior to proceed against "illegal" strikers by indicting them for the "crime of military rebellion." In 1962 the ILO committee ruled that many of the strikers had indeed been convicted for acts of armed rebellion rather than in the pursuit of trade union issues, and noted also that the government had limited the meaning of "military rebellion," excluding from that category strikes relating only to labor claims. Furthermore, some arrested strikers had been tried by a civil court and released. But even though it was conceded that there was a general loosening up in authoritarian-corporatist Spain, the ILO again requested the government to change its labor charter.

During 1962 and 1963 new waves of strikes broke out. And the Internationals filed new complaints, alleging that workers were being persecuted, arrested, tortured, and exiled, and protesting that the government was continuing to impose labor agreements on workers. Further, the Internationals demanded that an ILO Commission of Inquiry be sent to Spain to publicize these practices more widely. Again the committee was careful to distinguish between trade union grievances and acts of political rebellion, but it requested the Spanish government to guarantee civil trials for the accused, to make available copies of court judgments of convicted strikers, to ease the restrictions on the right to strike, and to institute conciliation procedures for industrial disputes. And again the government responded, sending some trial transcripts, removing the cases of strikers from the jurisdiction of military courts, and claiming that certain kinds of strikes were now being permitted. Nevertheless, the complainants, now joined by the IFCTU, continued to press for a full-scale international inquiry. The Spanish government, it should be recalled, was at this time trying to overhaul its economy, to allow new initiatives to private business, to attract foreign capital, and to "rejoin Europe" economically by way of some kind of association with the Common Market. The Spanish authorities charged with economic development, if no one else in the government, were well aware that the practices of a repressive-corporatist state were wholly incompatible with these objectives, and should therefore be removed.

And the break came in 1965. Following the 1964 strikes in the Basque provinces, the government instituted freely elected workers' and employers' councils, which seemed likely to develop into collective bargaining agents. At the same time it allowed more collective agreements to be concluded, and amended the penal code to permit the right to strike. In response, the committee noted these developments and agreed once more that some of the trade unionists arrested were indeed guilty of acts resembling sedition. But it continued to press for still more extensive amendments to the penal code and the Labor Charter in order to free unions from the shadow of arbitrary treatment and military repression; it also insisted that the Ministry of Economics give up its power of reviewing and withholding approval of collective agreements. As additional allegations of the persecution of trade unionists arrived in Geneva in 1966 and 1967, the committee continued to score the Spanish government for the gap between the basic ILO principles and the evolving Spanish institutions, even as it noted that Spanish civil court decisions were increasingly protecting the rights of workers.

In 1967, taking advantage of the expulsion from Spain of an ICFTU official who had sought to help detained Spanish colleagues, the committee suggested high-level conversations between the government, the ILO, and the Internationals as a "friendly" way to discuss the tangled web of issues. This suggestion was accepted by the Spanish government and endorsed by the 1968 session of the International Labor Conference. It is worth noting that the mission is a "study group," made up of three ILO-appointed experts, not the official Fact-Finding and Conciliation Commission. Its members are to discuss the content of a new labor code now being drafted with Spanish authorities, who apparently hope by this means to legitimate Spain's reentry into the company of European nations.

Though the Spanish case is instructive and striking as an example of incremental compliance and value sharing, the circumstances surrounding it are fairly unique, so that there is little hope for wider emulation. Decaying, even senile, authoritarian states beset internally with reform-minded bureaucrats are not common occurrences. In many superficially similar states, there is no infrastructure of voluntary groups with clear objectives and organizational experience; hence advantage cannot always be taken of the help extended by interested Internationals. And the desire to rejoin a larger cultural grouping is not a typical aspiration, particularly when doing so means in effect renouncing one's own past.

The Case of Greece. Enough has been said of the conditions in Greece since 1950 to make a description of the legal and institutional strictures on trade unions unnecessary. Though the officially sanctioned and government-subsidized trade union structure did not come into conflict with the various post–civil war governments, individual unions and unionists most certainly did. A flood of complaints streamed into Geneva in unprecedented numbers, largely the work of national unions disadvantaged by the official structure. Some of the efforts were supported by the WFTU, which entered its own complaints as well. The communist International won its first victory in Greece with a 1961 ILO decision requesting the government to change the procedure permitting prefects to remove trade union officers and giving "public security committees" various discretionary competences over unions.[19]

A major change in the Greek political climate, characterized before by a post–civil war insecurity (a sensitivity that was indulged until 1958 by the ILO), came with the election of the Center Union government in 1963, and especially after its reelection in 1964. As part of that government's plans for a moderate "opening toward the Left," some thought was given to changing the restrictions on trade unions. Certain ministries were anxious to amend the laws and regulations that had occasioned so much dissatisfaction, though the cabinet apparently was far from unanimous on the issue, and various groups on the Right strongly opposed any relaxation. Nevertheless, the new government proceeded with its plans, triggering a chain of events that culminated in the Fact-Finding and Conciliation Commission assuming an important role. Moreover, the situation resulted in the dispatch of a formal Commission of Inquiry, the first and only time such a commission was sent at the behest of trade unionists rather than a government. The sequence of events was as follows.

The Center Union Party, while still in opposition, had unsuccessfully wooed the leadership of the Greek General Confederation of Labor and its general secretary, F. Makris. Upon being rebuffed, the party then attempted to build up support among various trade unions and to split them off from the GGCL. Once elected, moreover, the new government, headed by George Papandreou, withdrew subventions that had been given to "loyal" trade unions since the end of the civil war and, according to Makris, proceeded to subsidize its own supporters instead, at the same time announcing its intention of gradually moving toward a completely autonomous union structure, financed solely by union members. Further, the government enacted Legislative Decree 4361, which (1) eliminated almost all government supervision over unions and (2) compelled unions to revise their bylaws in such a fashion as to democratize union elections, prevent fraud and inequitable representation in federations and conventions, and penalize unions financed solely by government subsidies. Most important of all, the decree so defined both the term of office for union officials and the requirements for calling a general meeting for the election of officers as to make the future tenure of the existing GGCL leadership extremely dubious. Expecting to be ousted, Makris and his colleagues filed a complaint with the Committee on Freedom of Association in September 1964, alleging that Convention 87 had been violated because the new decree stipulated the content of union bylaws. The Greek government, in response to the complaint, spontaneously and almost immediately requested that the case be referred to the Fact-Finding and Conciliation Commission. The committee, meanwhile, had recognized the gravity of the charge because of the alleged imposition of union bylaws.[20]

A commission panel, headed by Erik Dreyer (a high Danish civil servant), was appointed and sworn in; it held its first meeting in Geneva in July 1965. At that time arrangements were made to receive depositions, to invite spokesmen and witnesses for both parties, and to otherwise attempt to "find facts." The evidence was to be reviewed at the panel's next session, prior to a scheduled conciliation visit to Greece. In the meantime, the march of events in Greece had not come to a halt. The Center Union government was overthrown in July 1965, to be followed by three governments of a much more conservative color. Nevertheless, as predicted, Makris and his colleagues on the GGCL Executive were dismissed as a result of the Papandreou decree. However, no agreement could be reached on their successors as union factions began fighting among themselves and sought court annulments of their rivals' appointments. One judicial intervention after another resulted in a massive game of musical chairs among union officials—though the redoubtable Makris was not one of the players.

While the situation was still fluid, the ILO received a communication, on June 8, 1966, on behalf of Makris. In it he withdrew his complaint and explained that, thanks to the efforts of the commission, the relationship between the GGCL and the government was much improved, and Decree 4361 had not turned out to be such a formidable anti-labor weapon after all. The Dreyer panel then addressed a query to the government, which confirmed that relations had improved, and that the provisions of the decree were no longer at issue, though there were no plans afoot to amend it. After careful inquiry, the commission at its second session, in July 1966, decided to close the case and not to proceed to the conciliation phase.[21] Immediately thereafter, Makris once again became general secretary of the GGCL. Moreover, the stream of complaints from Greek unions resumed, suggesting that no major reforms had been carried out, despite government assurances.

After April 1967, with the overthrow of parliamentary democracy by the military dictatorship, a new element was added: conservatives and reformers alike became the victims of repression, and Makris once more found it desirable to appeal to Geneva. In addition, the three large Internationals submitted a joint complaint, attacking the very principle of military controls over unions and raising the whole nexus of issues as a human rights case. These charges led to a prompt condemnation by the committee, but they brought no response from the Greek government.[22] However, the next step did.

During the summer of 1968, three West European worker delegates and the Czech worker delegate to the International Labor
Conference, in separate actions, demanded that an official Commission of Inquiry be sent to Greece in an effort to expose the repressive policies of the military regime. Such a mission, organized
under Article 26 of the ILO Constitution, represents the most
formal and official sanction available to the organization. At the
time of writing, the commission had not submitted its report on
the state of freedom of association. However, there is at least an
indication of some insecurity on the part of the Greek military, for
the commission was allowed into the country and formal cooperation was extended.

This entire sequence of events raises a number of questions.
Why did the Greek government, the target of ILO criticism for
five years or more, suddenly become very responsive in 1964 and
again in 1968? Why, if Decree 4361 illustrates the extent of responsiveness, did the Papandreou government suggest recourse to
the Fact-Finding and Conciliation Commission instead of taking
its chances with the milder procedure? Why did the military government accept the Commission of Inquiry? And, finally, what
significance does the withdrawal of the 1964 complaint before the
completion of the conciliation procedure have for value sharing?

Unlike its many predecessors, the Center Union government was
genuinely concerned with major economic and social reforms in
Greece. Like many precariously established democratic regimes
before it, the new government sought additional legitimacy in
order to stave off its domestic enemies, and found it in an internationally sanctioned procedure: the government could and did cite
its obligations to the ILO as a reason for overhauling the trade
union system and making it autonomous of the state. Under the
circumstances, then, it is both instructive and ironic that Case 413
represents a protest of the workers' leadership against a regime
seeking to democratize the system of government-sponsored trade
unionism. The plain fact is, the leaders were fighting for their jobs;
the real issue was simply *who* was going to run the unions—as was
clearly established by the alacrity with which the ousted leaders

made their peace with the provisions of the controversial decree, once they were reinstalled in office.

Granting that the government was anxious to rid itself of the old leadership, why did it find it necessary to suggest that the ILO resort to the elaborate and formal fact-finding procedure? Even as the conciliation process was going forward, the commission took pains to commend the parties for their newfound agreement on the rules governing union elections—thus implicitly approving of the rules despite the government's role in defining the content of union bylaws. Similarly, the commission wholeheartedly endorsed the move to abolish government subsidies to unions, at the same time acknowledging that some form of transitional financial support might be necessary until membership dues were sufficient to maintain the machinery. True, the Papandreou government had no way of foreseeing such an overwhelmingly favorable response to its policy. The best guess is that the government felt it would derive additional legitimacy from the most public and most authoritative international investigation possible, even though much the same decision might have been obtained if the matter had remained in the more discreet hands of the Committee on Freedom of Association.

Clearly, the Papandreou government intended to comply almost completely with past ILO requests to change law and practice, the protests of the union leaders notwithstanding, and saw in the Fact-Finding and Conciliation Commission a technique for mobilizing international support against domestic opponents. The three succeeding cabinets appear to have been uncertain about eventual implementation, since they did not rescind the crucial decree. Only with the coup of 1967 did the wheel come full circle; the military, in again ousting Makris, undid the previous progress. Nevertheless, they, in turn, felt compelled to bend to the storm of criticism in Europe, and so accepted the Commission of Inquiry.

The Fact-Finding and Conciliation Commission, in terminating the procedure prematurely, said that it felt the time had come to shift from the international to the national level, in order to facilitate further negotiations between government and unions. In a sense, the commission had no choice: there is nothing to conciliate when the parties concerned insist there is no dispute; parties must give evidence of "spontaneous consent." But in conceding the point, the commission may have established two important procedural precedents.

Does a complainant's withdrawal of charges automatically imply the end of an international effort at conciliation? The commission's answer was "no." Though in this particular case the commission found that spontaneous consent was indeed lacking, it did so only after closely questioning both parties, in effect declaring that such a finding can be made only after the commission assures itself the complainant acted freely and without threat. Still, the reassertion of the doctrine of spontaneous consent, we must admit, brings us right back to the legal position that was revealed in 1950, when the Fact-Finding and Conciliation machinery was created and was prevented from assuming a role.

Must the machinery limit its activities to giving satisfaction to the parties? Again, the commission's answer was in the negative (though it must be accepted with an eye to the realities of international value conflict). Whereas *conciliation* was held to depend on the general agreement of the parties, *fact finding* was held to be a public inquiry into general principles and their application, an inquiry that is not limited to the specific interest of the parties but is, rather, of worldwide concern. Hence the fact-finding phase cannot be terminated simply at the request of the parties.

The Case of Japan. However interesting the cases of Spain and Greece, it is the Japanese case that best demonstrates both the optimal role a combination of national and international pressures plays in lending authority to the international procedure for the protection of freedom of association and the rather sharp limits within which the process operates. Something must first be said about the background of Japan's industrial relations and sensitivity to international opinion.[23]

Japan joined the ILO in 1919, not because she was interested in freedom of association and labor rights, but because she sought legitimacy and recognition in international politics. Domestic labor policy during the 1920s and 1930s was based on the principle of co-opting radical and politicized unions through paternal-istic legislation; the government had no intention of recognizing unions as equal negotiating partners in collective bargaining. When the unions sought help from the ILO in the early years, they succeeded only to the extent of gaining informal recognition in appointing the labor delegate to the ILO. The government was content to use its membership in the organization to demonstrate its progressiveness and its sensitivity to the continuing Western charge of "social dumping," i.e., the *de facto* subsidizing of ex-ports through abnormally low wages and social security costs. This concern was to survive. During and after the American occupation, unions grew rapidly and autonomously, allying themselves for the most part with the Socialist Party. In the frequent fissures and fusions of that volatile group, the bulk of the unions, under the leadership of the main national federation (Sōhyō), affiliated with the left-wing socialists. After a short interlude during the "demo-cratization" phase accompanying the United States occupation, the political powers of the unions were restricted by law in order to oblige them, as in the American model, to devote themselves to trade union pursuits. Employees in the public sector were espe-cially restricted. Though some occupation laws were softened in 1952, the Liberal-Democratic government strengthened others in 1953, notably legislation prohibiting public employees (including teachers, railway and post office personnel, and local and munici-pal employees) from striking and from collective bargaining. The Japanese unions, though still affiliated with the ICFTU, grew more militant, and obtained the support of the WFTU in filing a com-plaint against the government, challenging the legislation hamp-ering their political activities. Even though the complaint was couched in general and militant Cold War language, and coincided with various anti-communist measures taken in connection with the Korean War, it resulted in recommendations to change the law, a recommendation that was only partly implemented by the gov-ernment.[24] A follow-up complaint, with substantially the same al-legations, was dismissed with a recommendation to provide alter-native grievance procedures.

In 1957, apparently worried over Sōhyō's drift toward the

WFTU, the ICFTU began to take greater interest in the Japanese labor scene. Japanese unions were increasingly turning to economic issues, and hence more concerned with buttressing freedom of association in a political context in which they perceived themselves as the victims of a post-occupation "roll back," an attempt by the Liberal-Democratic majority to hamstring their negotiating prowess, especially in the public sector, with the restrictive legislation passed in 1948–52. The context included various aspects. Railwaymen, barred from striking, resorted to various extra-legel slowdown maneuvers and to interruptions of train traffic to secure their demands. Though the ministries of Labor and Local Autonomy and the railways were not unsympathetic to all union demands, the ministries of Transport and Finance were; various awards by conciliation boards went unimplemented while the government dismissed union leaders from their employment for violation of work rules. Much the same sequence of events occurred in the postal service. Teachers, however, concerned with preventing the Ministry of Education from dominating school curriculum questions, demanded bargaining rights at the national and local levels that would enable them to push their political ideas in the context of curriculum development. Again, various ministries and agencies in the government disagreed with each other. These developments, it must be stressed, took place in a context in which public opinion strongly favored the government, though many intellectuals sided with the unions.

In 1958 the ICFTU joined the major unions in the public sector in filing Case 179. The legal issues can be summarized briefly. Japan had ratified Convention 98, but not the more elaborate and demanding Convention 87. The issues centered on: (1) the right of public employees to strike; (2) the right of union leaders to retain their union jobs (and membership), even if they were dismissed from government service; (3) the "full-time union officer" system enabling union officers to maintain their employee status and the associated benefits; and (4) the right of teachers to bargain collectively with the Ministry of Education on all issues, even though technically their "employers" were local authorities and school boards. Convention 98, the government argued stoutly, guaranteed none of these things.

Why was the issue internationalized by the Japanese unions in 1957? Sōhyō apparently enlisted the ICFTU in the struggle because of its own signal lack of success in the face of public opposition and a solid Liberal-Democratic majority in the Diet. Short of raising the issue of meeting international obligations—a sensitive issue in post-1945 Japan—there seemed to be no possibility of escalating the issue. And without escalation, there seemed to be no democratic way of stopping the "roll back" legislation. But why did the Japanese government finally respond, albeit over many years (1958–64), to the continuing onslaught of inquiries from the ILO? In the first place, there were ministries and government organs in Japan that wished to challenge the preeminence of the Ministry of Finance, and therefore sided, in varying degrees, with the unions. Further, certain factions in the Liberal-Democratic Party feared that the growing power of the unions could not be restrained with special legislation, and proposed instead that unions be brought into the structure of post-1945 Japanese democracy. Finally, and perhaps most importantly, the highest circles of the Liberal-Democratic Party included some who were sensitive to the charge heard in various international organizations, notably GATT (General Agreement on Tariffs and Trade), that Japan's restrictive labor practices looked suspiciously like social dumping. We should note that this charge had some currency at the very time Japan was making its spectacular economic recovery and hoped to seal its comeback in world trade with full membership in GATT.

Though the government proved responsive in some ways, it also temporized. It repeatedly promised to accede to ILO wishes and ratify Convention 87, but somehow it delayed putting legislation before the Diet to remove the disputed provisions from the 1948–52 laws. Moreover, when bills for the ratification of Convention 87 and the removal of the offensive provisions were finally introduced in 1960, they were accompanied by new provisions that the unions interpreted as an attempt to maintain the status quo. Meanwhile, various efforts at national fact-finding and conciliation went on, and suits continued to be brought before the courts, none leading to a resolution of the situation. As internationalization warmed the temperature of debate, Japan offered, in 1964, to receive the Fact-Finding and Conciliation Commission and to avail herself of its services, in order to show her loyalty to international obligations and her genuine desire to be progressive. During 1965 a three-man panel, again headed by Erik Dreyer, carried on the fact-finding phase of the procedure, plowing through the voluminous dossier of charges and countercharges, as well as the applicable Japanese legislation, in Geneva. Few new facts were turned up, one can assume, in view of the long history of ILO inquiry and the numerous efforts already undertaken by various Japanese governmental and quasi-governmental organs. Later that year, the panel went to Japan to try its hand at conciliation. It met with representatives of all parties, unions, and ministries, and listened to their charges once more, seeking to discover some minimum common ground among them. In that sense, the panel certainly negotiated with the antagonists, just as any conciliator would. But this is probably the first time in history that a panel born out of a general and permanent international complaint procedure had a chance to do so.

The issue facing the panel, then, was not the ratification of Convention 87 so much as it was the package of legislation that ought to accompany the ratification. What did the Dreyer committee propose? It stressed (as indeed many Japanese commentators had before) that what was most needed was to establish mutual trust between the unions and the government, which once achieved would permit the parties to negotiate directly, without exclusive reliance on parliamentary wrangling and action. Thus, instead of stressing the sanctity of international obligations, the committee made its main task the creation of a receptive climate within the Japanese cultural context; to that end it proposed a tripartite negotiating body be established to take up the disputed pieces of labor reform that had not yet passed the Diet. In the main reform-minded, the committee was nevertheless careful not to say so unequivocally, appreciating the government's concern for the stability and reliability of the public services involved. As things worked out, each side claimed that the Dreyer committee's recommendations were in its favor and at the same time gave due consideration to Japanese special conditions, no mean feat for a conciliator. Yet of the four major legal issues, only one was resolved: the right of union leaders to hold their union positions after dismissal from their jobs was affirmed.

Convention 87 was now painlessly ratified, but little else was accomplished. The tripartite panel recommended by the Dreyer committee duly met, but by 1968 it disbanded, having failed to make any headway on the issues. The "roll-back" legislation was only slightly amended, though the government made no effort to enforce the disputed provisions with consistency and rigor. It is still possible, of course, that this partial implementation will become a fuller victory for the unions once a real sense of mutual trust develops.

7. The Future

We must now put our findings to use in exploring the future of an international sharing of human rights values. We must summarize what functional analysis can teach us about the relevance of the functional strategy, and pinpoint where and why this admittedly second-best approach differs from the analysis of more optimistic observers, committed to a direct attack. Hence we must juxtapose a functional analysis of the UN's human rights activities to the optimists' more sweeping approach, especially with respect to such additions to the UN armory as a Commissioner on Human Rights and the convention eliminating racial discrimination. Finally, we must ask ourselves how well the future cause of human rights is served by a legal doctrine that seeks to side-step the notion of consent in its urge to generalize and universalize human freedom directly.

NEO-FUNCTIONALISM AND INTERNATIONAL CONSENSUS

The strategy the ILO has followed in seeking to establish freedom of association conforms, in general, to the rules of neo-functionalism.[1] To explore the success of that strategy, this study has made use of neo-functional analysis, specifically in our hypotheses concerning the ILO machinery and the behavior of its clients. There are, in our overall findings, elements favoring the progressive sharing of limited values, capable of gradual diffusion; but there are also many signs suggesting failure. In short, the neo-functional strategy, despite its modest expectations and built-in qualifications, cannot in any sense be considered a significant success.

The findings supporting the utility of the strategy are: human rights are increasingly made the objects of complaints; voluntary organizations at the national level manifest a growing concern; the legitimacy of the supervisory machinery is developing nicely, as are its methods of inquiry; the scope of rights to be protected is gradually expanding; the earlier situation, in which a disproportionately large number of democratic regimes were the victims of complaints is yielding to one in which authoritarian regimes are more and more often defendants; and the distorting influence of international, politically charged issues is being more and more pushed to the side.

But some of our other findings, on points even more necessary for global value sharing, fail to bear out the utility of a functional strategy: the authority of the international machinery is not improving; the overall record of national compliance is very poor and shows no signs of improvement; compliance is concentrated among countries least in need of international prodding, whereas those most in need remain uniformly unresponsive.

The future seems to hold no great hope of a change in the pattern. If we are right in postulating that the optimal conditions for even a faulty working of the functional processes of value sharing are to be found in new democracies in the early stages of economic development and in shaky authoritarian systems needing external support to speed their own transformation, then the limits of the process are also suggested. Among the new democracies, the likely candidates for future responsiveness to ILO pressure are Colombia and Costa Rica; Greece, Brazil, and Portugal stand out among the authoritarian regimes as those that are likely to undergo evolution and possess a core of interest groups able and willing to assume the role assigned to them by functional theory.

Not surprisingly, our somber conclusion is not a popular or widely accepted view; witness the effusive and sanguine opinions and expectations cited in the beginning of this study. Moreover, the contrary view seems to command more respect. Those who hold it claim we are living in a period of unprecedented change in the time-hallowed ways of life everywhere, especially in the Third

World.[2] They argue that demands for equality, dignity, respect, well-being, and a recognition of the aspirations of common people are heard the world over—in short, that a global revolution is under way. "Its aims, and the great social forces that have swept over government throughout the world, have largely centered on human rights. Whether they will turn out to be genuine revolutions, or only transfers of power from one group to another, cannot be known at present, but . . . the rest of the century will witness the consolidation and establishment of human rights at a rate that no other historical epoch has ever experienced."[3] How can this view be squared with our analysis of the modest success enjoyed by the right of freedom of association?

The contemporary revolution in human rights seeks collective benefits, generalized benefits, abstract moral values. It is less concerned with protecting the individual or the "selfish" group against the state, the nation, or "the people," than it is with safeguarding the collectivity's right to equality, dignity, and a rising standard of living. Freedom is perceived as the collective achievement of such a program, a program designed to banish the foes of human rights: feudalism, tribalism, traditionalism, and capitalism, together with the exploiting classes that allegedly animate those social systems.

To see a worldwide revolution of rising demands everywhere does not entitle us to claim that the rights of those who are making the revolution have actually been safeguarded against the next wave of social claimants. That would require precisely the kinds of steps insisted on in the ILO procedure for protecting freedom of association. It is difficult to see how, in logic, a *program* for human betterment can be mistaken for institutional measures that would make such a program workable and permanent. To raise standards of living, to free women from bondage, to resettle refugees, to eliminate foreign capitalists is not to create permanent rights that ensure individual and group participation in the political and economic life of a country; institutions for curbing the state must also be provided. Today we have widespread demands for human betterment without any concomitant commitment to check arbitrary state power.

The nub of the paradox is the rate of change at different *levels* of action. What happens at the international level, as initiated by international organizations, is poorly geared to what goes on at the state level. And this finding is crucial for our inquiry concerning the progressive sharing of values internationally. Various revolutions in aspirations and mass values are undeniably in progress—at the level of national political action. But at that level values differ appreciably; a commitment to betterment does *not* necessarily imply an increase of individual and group power at the expense of state power. On the international level, however, the UN and the specialized agencies seek to protect human rights through institutionalized means—that is, to promote the rights of individuals and groups through an international supervisory and complaint machinery. A similar definition of norms and the supervision of their implementation—which are inseparable operations—are something quite different from the programmatic assertion of new rights to dignity and welfare at the national level. It is thus possible to witness dramatic and even revolutionary change nationally in which the institutions of the international system have no active part. Change, in short, is not only taking place at a different rate on the national level; it is also taking a different path, both normatively and institutionally. Hence a sharing of values is by no means assured, or even likely.

Domestic value change is proceeding autonomously from international activity; it is going on more rapidly and it professes qualitatively different values. For changes initiated at the international level to gain acceptance at the national level, the cooperation of mobilized, domestic political forces is required. A second requirement is that the government concerned be committed to values compatible with those elaborated at the international level. As we have seen, neither requirement is met very often in practice. Most governments and societies are adopting programs that are not congruent with UN activity in the human rights field, though such programs might well be in accord with UN economic development and planning activities. So far the two levels of activity have not been brought into harmony.[4] In fact, the global enthusiasm for human rights originated in the context of decolonization, in the overwhelming consensus favoring the abolition of colonialism, racism, and discrimination. Governments that enthusiastically joined this consensus—especially in Africa, the Middle East, and South and Southeast Asia—may not be equally enthusiastic about limiting their own freedom of action when it is a question of their own citizens rather than of racism in someone else's country. Indeed, the record of compliance with ILO requests on the part of these regimes suggests that no great enthusiasm for this kind of value sharing is likely to prevail.

More optimistic observers than I tend to meet these judgments by calling attention to counter-trends. They admit that the international discussion of human rights may be replete with ritual posturing, that many governments do in fact deplore an opponent's practices without any intention of changing their own. But they would argue that such rhetoric can have a cumulative effect, that it can in the end arouse the conscience of a government, making it face issues at home it would otherwise ignore. To this I would answer, that the prick of conscience is felt primarily in democratic countries, and that in those countries international criticism merely serves as an added stimulus. It is also suggested that though there is no deep and unified global commitment to international human rights protection on the part of governments, there is such a commitment to international organizations. According to this argument, as UN agencies are called on to increase their activities in the fields of economic and social development, they can include measures for the protection of human rights in the package of services and obligations offered to the recipients of that aid. Sometimes, moreover, the recipients will prefer to commit themselves to a new policy of respecting rights by accepting a UN text or declaration simply because this seems to them a more legitimate course of action than merely acceding to domestic political pressure or implied threats from international agencies. In short, these observers think it possible that the next major breakthrough in increased UN authority in the economic and social development field—a breakthrough that is almost certain to occur—will be accompanied by an increase in authority for human rights programs.

Again I must differ. In my judgment, governments are very adept
at separating contexts and programs. As long as they can be reasonably certain of obtaining economic and social benefits from the
UN in any event, they will be wary about accepting additional
obligations that run counter to national policy; they have no need
to bargain over issues.

We should not confuse the apparent blossoming of a concern
for the international protection of human rights in certain regions
of the world for a genuine breakthrough toward global conscious-
ness. It is certainly true that there has been an impressive development of shared norms, and of institutions for their protection, in
Western Europe since 1950. Though the European Commission on
Human Rights has been extremely cautious in pronouncing governments guilty of alleged violations of the European Convention
on Human Rights, and though the European Court on Human
Rights has heard only three cases in its history, the fact remains
that government responsiveness to the machinery is exemplary
(with the notable exception of Greece). The story in the Western
Hemisphere is equally interesting. There, an Inter-American Commission on Human Rights has emerged as an autonomous agency
not subject to governmental manipulation, the unforeseen consequence of a largely rhetorical gesture. The commission, established
by the Organization of American States when sanctions were imposed against the Dominican Republic and Cuba, proceeded to act
as if it had a sweeping mandate and began to consider complaints
of individuals against their governments, even though there is no
inter-American convention defining human rights. Still, despite the
commission's continued aggressiveness, it cannot be claimed that
governments have been particularly responsive, either in acceding
to the commission's requests for information and permission to
make on-the-spot inquiries, or in accepting its suggestions for
changes in law or in practice.[5]

Two further points need to be made about the regional machinery. First, its norms are of the Western civil libertarian variety
and are designed to protect the individual against arbitrary state
power. That is to say, the values being shared are traditional West-

ern values rather than the concept of collective freedom more current in the Third World. Hence European and Western Hemisphere trends run counter to trends elsewhere. Second, the very
fact that this machinery was set up and plays an increasingly important role reinforces our thesis that we are living in an era of
growing value conflict, of increasing world divergence over basic
norms for man, society, and the state. The assertion and invocation of individual rights in the regional machinery contrasts
sharply with UN practice. Far from contributing to the sharing
of values globally, then, the regional systems underscore the evolution—perhaps temporarily—of diverging norms.

An unfriendly environment would thus seem to doom a progressive sharing of values through legal and political means, as incor-
porated in UN texts now in the drafting stage or awaiting entry
into force. It does not much matter whether we think that the definition of legal norms will trigger opinion and value change, or
whether we feel that educational efforts should be made first to
change opinion at the national level, with value change and formalization following later. International law, including most UN conventions and declarations, is still subject to strictures that limit
it as an instrument of social change. As Stanley Hoffman tells us:

The nature of the international system condemns international law to
all the weaknesses and perversions that it is so easy to deride. International law is merely a magnifying mirror that reflects faithfully and
cruelly the essence and the logic of international politics. In a frag-
mented world there is no "global perspective" from which anyone can
authoritatively assess, endorse, or reject the separate national efforts
at making international law serve national interest above all. Like the
somber universe of Albert Camus' Caligula, this is a judgeless world
where no one is innocent.[6]

Must it also be a hopeless world, the world of Jean Paul Sartre,
from which there is no exit?

LAW, OPINION, AND FUTURE UN POLICY

Before we commit ourselves to the finality of existentialist doom,
we ought to examine some of the major policy steps now being
debated by the members of the UN. Clearly, those who would put

their faith in the process of drafting conventions and declarations are in for one disappointment after another. At best, that process will continue to be a rhetorical exercise, linked to international value confrontation rather than to genuine value sharing. Not that confrontation cannot lead to sharing; it can, but to do so the rate of change at the international and national levels, as well as the expectations at both levels, would have to be more nearly in phase. In the meantime, UN debate more often than not resembles the proverbial dialogue of the deaf. And at worst, the process of legal-diplomatic drafting will lead to a premature formalization of norms that lack a clientele. Premature formalization is positively undesirable from the point of view of value sharing: it leads to frustration and disappointment in all international law, to the very cynicism and exaggerated rejection that prevails in so many places today.

But what about a more selective process, one in which conventions and supervisory machinery are provided for limited purposes and specific client groups? What if, in this process, legal texts are prepared with an eye to the functional approach to law, to the virtues of vague drafting and of loosely defined competences for supervisory organs? Functional jurisprudence might aid the process of value sharing by enunciating single, normative objectives that have wide support and specific client groups, thus permitting the legal-political drama of invocation, complaint, inquiry, and interpretation to follow its inherent logic—incremental expansion in scope and growing specificity.[7] Freedom of association seemed an obvious candidate for this process, and its record as a catalyst of value sharing reflects successes as well as failures, despite a hostile international environment. Are there other examples showing a similar evolution? Can the process continue—or even become more widespread?

In the early years of the League of Nations, the protection of national minorities provided an analogous field of action: specific and articulate client groups abounded; internationally guaranteed norms, of the deliberate ambiguity favored by functional jurisprudence, were more than ample; and a formal supervisory machinery was created in the League Council and the Secretariat. The machinery "worked" in the sense that complaints were processed and decisions were usually carried out. But the sharing of values among Germans and Poles, Hungarians and Rumanians, Lithuanians and Poles was hardly conspicuous! Some contemporary commentators noted that the League system actually discouraged the sharing of values by the majority and the protected minority, in that it provided the legal and institutional means for shielding groups from one another instead of stimulating them to mingle and learn to live together. Moreover, the entire machinery collapsed quickly, without a whimper from the international community, with a drastic change in the international system, i.e., when Germany withdrew from the League and France's system of alliances in Eastern Europe broke down.[8]

Is the same fate in store for the machinery associated with the Anti-Discrimination Convention, the next-best candidate for a successful functional jurisprudence in sight? The supervisory and complaint machinery created under the UN convention is certainly no stronger or more explicit than the machinery provided for the protection of freedom of association in 1950. If some ambiguity in the scope and meaning is indeed desirable in a modest legal approach, this text meets the requirement. Further, the requirement of client groups is also met; there are such groups in many countries, even though they are not yet organized into Internationals. Though the convention does not explicitly authorize group complaints, little legal ingenuity would be needed to accommodate them, particularly since there is not much likelihood of a recourse to the ICJ in the projected procedure. In fact, the standing committee and the ad hoc commissions provided in the convention look very much like the somewhat shadowy organs available to the ILO in 1950. If governments prove to be unable to resist the temptation of using the complaint procedure to embarrass their ideological opponents (e.g., Arab nations against Israel, Cuba against the United States, Korea against Japan), no legal or institutional evolution is likely to take place, and value sharing will remain as elusive as it is now. But implementation and other signs of governmental responsiveness might be expected if complaints are brought by individuals and groups rather than by governments, since obvious politicization could thereby be avoided. Furthermore, it is at least conceivable that even non-ratifying countries would be exposed to international inquiry if the supervisory organs were to insist that Articles 55 and 56 of the UN Charter create definite obligations, much as the ILO successfully cited the ILO Constitution to proceed against ILO members that were not parties to Conventions 87 and 98.[9] In short, countries that proved to be responsive to ILO pressure, or in tune with internationally supported values capable of being shared, are subject to the same forces in the context of the Anti-Discrimination Convention.

Does this projection ignore changes in the international system, such as doomed the League of Nations' attempt to protect national minorities? The international system is tending neither toward bipolarity nor toward tripolarity. Nor is a clustering of all international issues around a single pole of power or ideology likely. Instead, we can expect a world in which many blocs coexist and in which there is a splintering of issues into combinations that do not necessarily coincide with bloc objectives.[10] The setting, in sum, favors the evolution of international measures against racial discrimination, and the modest sharing of common values implicit in that process.

Turning to the UN Commission on Human Rights, in view of that body's history of restricting its own competence in investigating alleged violations of various UN pronouncements, it seems unlikely to play a strong role in encouraging value sharing. As of 1968, the commission had received tens of thousands of complaints from individuals and non-governmental groups, charging many nations with violations of the Universal Declaration. To this writing, no investigation or systematic discussion of these complaints has taken place; instead the Secretary-General has been asked simply to catalog them under the rubrics suggested by the Universal Declaration, without publicizing the results. Nor have the member nations shown much interest in strengthening the machinery. This became clear in 1968, when the Sub-Commission on

Discrimination, charged by ECOSOC with investigating complaints of "gross" violations of human rights and situations in which there was a "constant pattern" of violations, reported to the full commission that such violations had taken place in Greece and Haiti. The commission declined to act.*

Furthermore, various nonlegal projects the commission has undertaken in an effort to create a climate of opinion favoring the eventual acceptance of legal norms are slow to show results. Apparently member nations have little desire to avail themselves of technical assistance to further human rights. True, government officials are increasingly inclined to accept fellowships and training opportunities in the field. But in the regional seminars held for other officials, the tendency has been to concentrate on technical issues or

* For further details, see Richard B. Bilder, "Rethinking International Human Rights: Some Basic Questions," *Wisconsin Law Review*, 1969, 1, p. 184. The commissions declined to act because of objections from the Haitian, Greek, and Soviet delegates. Moreover, the sub-commission's membership was increased to 26 nations, with the new appointees overwhelmingly non-Western and hostile to a strengthened and impartial complaint machinery. During the 1969 session of the commission, the new mandate was used only to castigate Israel's treatment of the Arab population in the occupied territories. The commission voted to establish a special Working Group of Experts with power to investigate, receive communications, hear witnesses, and "use such modalities of procedure" as it deemed necessary to check on violations by Israel of the Geneva Convention on the Protection of Civilian Persons in Time of War (1949). The resolution was adopted by a vote of 13 to one, with 16 abstentions. Support was confined to the socialist nations, the Arab countries, and other Afro-Asian nations with Islamic ties. See Commission on Human Rights, *Report on the 25th Session*, UN doc. E/4621, E/CN. 4/1007, pp. 66–76.

The commission was also shown the Secretary-General's catalog of "communications" received from individuals and groups alleging violations of human rights. The following description of commission action is indicative of the "enthusiastic" interest of governments in impartially examining such complaints: "The Secretary-General distributed to the members of the Commission a confidential list of communications, replies of Governments and a confidential document of a statistical nature. In conformity with Economic and Social Council resolution 1235 (XLII) of 6 June 1967, copies of the communications ... were made available to the members of the Commission. A non-confidential list of communications containing a brief indication of the substance of each communication, however addressed, which dealt with the principles involved in the promotion of universal respect for, and observance of, human rights was also distributed. The Commission did not consider this item because of lack of time" (*ibid.*, p. 173).

to argue about the agenda. And as indicated earlier, the system of triennial reporting is an out-and-out failure.[11] It would take an untold length of time for opinion at the national level to be changed in a uniform and shared manner on the basis of this program.

The major new development in the international protection of human rights is the current proposal to appoint a High Commissioner for Human Rights. The novelty of this proposal lies in the straddling of rival approaches, notably as between those who argue for legal formalization and those who argue for domestic opinion change as initial steps. Is this new instrument likely to advance the international sharing of values on certain basic human rights more effectively than supervisory mechanisms provided by specific conventions?

The proposal, as of 1968 approved only by the Commission on Human Rights and ECOSOC, envisages a UN officer who will be concerned with all the rights covered in the Universal Declaration and the International Covenants. In many respects his office would closely resemble the human rights commissions that have been established in the United States in the last few years.* If the present resolution is approved, the commissioner will not be empowered to adjudicate disputes, issue decisions, or even marshal adverse international publicity. One of his main functions will be to provide advice and assistance upon request to UN organs and to governments as well; hence he could act as mediator or conciliator in disputes among states involving human rights issues. Further, he is to report regularly to the General Assembly, keeping it in-

---

* My treatment relies mostly on William Korey, "The Key to Human Rights–Implementation," *International Conciliation*, No. 570 (November 1968), pp. 59–64. The High Commissioner is sometimes compared to an ombudsman. However, much depends on how that institution is understood. As originally conceived in Scandinavia, the ombudsman was to be a champion of the citizen against bureaucratic arbitrariness and neglect, charged with protecting the *legally established* rights of citizens. A similar role would not, strictly speaking, be possible for an international official if a delinquent state had not ratified various international conventions. More recently, the Scandinavian institution has become a medium for exposing general administrative malpractice and governmental inefficiency as well, a function performed in the United States by grand juries and clearly not possible for an international official.

formed of the extent to which member nations are carrying out UN resolutions, declarations, and conventions and adding his own best judgment on how problems preventing implementation might be overcome. These reports may be made after the commissioner has consulted governments; in short, cautious negotiations leading to quiet assurances that certain steps will be taken can become a part of the reporting function, thus adding another slight increment of international pressure. Finally and most importantly, the the commissioner is to have "access to the communications concerning human rights addressed to the United Nations [and could] whenever he deems it appropriate, bring them to the attention of the Government . . . to which any such communications explicitly refer."[12] This provision would enable him to take up some of the tens of thousands of complaints received—and filed—by the UN Commission on Human Rights.

We should note first of all that many UN members, including the socialist bloc, opposed this proposal, though it was strongly favored by the United States; in the absence of follow-through machinery and of autonomous groups at the national level, it seems unlikely that these complaints will be investigated. As for the device of reporting to the General Assembly, it seems no more promising with respect to resolutely delinquent countries than similar ILO practices.[13] Nor does the commissioner's advice and assistance seem more likely to be invoked than existing UN machinery in this field. That leaves us with the commissioner's powers of conciliation in disputes within and among nations. Here ILO experience in intra-national disputes is fairly impressive for certain kinds of regimes—Greece, Brazil, Chile, Spain, Japan, Great Britain. The ILO record in the cases of international disputes, however, is far more dubious.[14] Even under the best possible conditions, the new office is not likely to match the performance of the ILO machinery, since the High Commissioner will not have the benefit of the kind of intimate contact the trade union Internationals provide. Our data suggest that, given the present international environment, we can expect the commissioner's usefulness to be limited to protecting and encouraging groups and individuals in authoritarian regimes in the process of transforming themselves; and even then, only where there is some history of democracy and concern with civil liberties. In short, his contribution to universal value sharing is fated to be minimal, at least for now and the immediate future. At the most hopeful, we can expect that he may have some success in planting the seeds of a local concern with freedom, encouraging a growth that will blossom at a later stage in the evolution of the international system.

IS NATURAL LAW THE ONLY BASIS FOR VALUE SHARING?

UN programs for the protection of human rights rely on legal techniques of three major inspirations: (1) positive law of a general and sweeping kind, as in the International Covenants; (2) positive law of the functional kind, as in the ILO approach and the Anti-Discrimination Convention; and (3) natural law, as in the Universal Declaration and the General Assembly resolutions in support of it. We have attempted to show that, in the present international system, positive enactments of a general kind are at best self-defeating with respect to universal value sharing, and at worst hypocritically self-seeking. Further, we have sought to demonstrate that more limited functional enactments have gained some ground but can by no means be considered an unqualified success. There remains the possibility that value sharing might be advanced if the doctrine of state consent implicit in all positive law could be avoided. Hence arguments that stress a natural law basis for a concern with human rights must be examined in some detail, since natural law is by definition universal. If a valid basis for a human rights program could be discovered in natural law, we might with some justification conclude that even though the current international system is hostile to the progressive sharing of values, a later system would permit putatively established values to grow and prosper precisely because they have a basis in truly universal aspirations. The question then is: do human rights values in fact have such a basis?

At least one contemporary writer has categorically asserted that there is no basis in positive international law for a human rights program that stresses legal definition and enforcement.[15] But much depends on what we accept as the sources of that law. Clearly, if we focus on four of the traditionally accepted sources—treaties, custom, judicial precedent, and legal opinion—positive law offers little help to a truly universal human rights program. Treaties, the arch-positivist basis of obligations, create new norms only to the extent that they are accepted by states and faithfully implemented. "Custom in its legal sense," comments J. L. Brierly, "means something more than mere habit or usage; it is a usage felt *by those who follow it* to be an obligatory one."[16] This begs the question; it merely suggests that those who favor a given right create or follow a certain practice, but those who do not follow that practice are violating no rule or law. Judicial precedent and the opinions of text writers are very weak reeds on which to rely; divided in the past, there is no reason to suppose they will lead in one unequivocal direction as far as a worldwide effort is concerned. All four of these sources are based on consent: treaties and custom imply agreement on the part of the states subscribing to the specific rules of a treaty or the unwritten rules of usage; judicial precedent and legal texts imply agreement on which precedent is to be followed and which is to be rejected, on which text writer is to be held in top esteem and which is to be dismissed lightly. Positive international law, as the contractual consent of the governed, is indeed a poor basis for a human rights program aiming at universal values.

But there is a fifth accepted source of international law that is not based on consent: "the general principles of law recognized by civilized nations." If we assume that in our present global political system to be a UN member is to be recognized as a civilized nation, we are then in the presence of a universal *ius gentium.* Practices and principles observed in the municipal and private law of all or most nations become "general principles" to guide international legal action in an authoritative fashion. Let us grant that ILO organs have not invoked "general principles" in seeking to protect freedom of association, relying instead exclusively on treaties. Nor did the League of Nations in protecting national minorities. Nevertheless, some argue that "general principles" are certainly expressed in the General Assembly's ringing declarations against racism, colonialism, discrimination, and *apartheid.* These principles do not rest on a globally shared consensus of any depth. Are they sufficiently authoritative to serve as a source of law when the accepted positive sources fail because of a shallow substantive content?

To argue that they can brings us very close to natural law notions, to a view that sees imperatives, forces, and sources above and beyond the expressed will of men and governments, as formalized in legislation and administrative routine. Moreover, a natural law basis of globally shared human rights—in default of governmental consent—inheres in the objective social and economic conditions of world interdependence. Or so some writers would have us believe, at any rate. The pace of social differentiation everywhere creates widespread alienation, a condition that can be cured only with the help of "guidance mechanisms" for units larger than the all-but-helpless nation-states of our era. However, since most nations are conceded by these analysts to be living in a "tribal" frame of mind—despite professions of attachment to larger and global values—some supranational mechanism is needed to provide guidance; the objective existence of interdependence is not enough.[17]

Some see this mechanism at work in the sentiment of moral solidarity that unifies intellectuals and other members of national elites across national boundaries. Others see it as visible in the increasing use of universalistic arguments by governments seeking to legitimate purely particularistic acts abroad, the tribute vice is paying virtue. But for many the most important mechanism is the calling of the social scientist; his true ethos should be the realization in action of the universal aspect of his claim to knowledge: "to rely on the one foundation all social scientists, whatever their affiliations, can share and measure—values whose community is all men. Such values also provide the only immovable foundation: Tribes merge and split, but the community of man remains. This does entail a transcendental stand, as the realization of the community is lagging, but so do all other positions, with one difference—the global community is the only one which embraces all social scientists *and* all of their subjects."[18]

Let us assimilate into this argument two types of social scientists, judges and lawyers, and let us suppose that they make themselves the carriers of this ethos in the face of governmental conduct belying these values; let us suppose further that general principles of law result from this activity, principles that must of necessity have the visionary quality of natural law, as does the clarion call to action sounded to social science.

Hence we must turn to non-consensual doctrines if we wish to find a metabehavioral basis for universal value sharing through human rights programs. The Nuremberg Judgment provides such a doctrine because of its incorporation of the right to be protected against "crimes against humanity," a category that is wholly consistent with natural law tradition, but did not formally exist prior to 1945. The discussion on the occasion of the adoption of the genocide convention suggests that it fits the same pattern. But are these true examples of a creation of non-consensual norms by a special elite? The facts argue otherwise. The crime of genocide was defined by governments (or at least by government lawyers), the definition was voted on by governments, and the treaty was ratified by governments. The concept of "crimes against humanity" was created in the same way following World War II, when the victorious powers established the Nuremberg Tribunal. How then can it be considered non-consensual? The sequence of events was clearly based on the explicit consent of the victors, a consent that as yet has not been concurred in by the community of nations at large: similar "crimes" have been committed since, have gone unpunished, *and* have often even gone unchallenged.

Still, the ICJ itself has asserted there are principles relating to human rights that "are recognized by civilized states as binding on states *even without any conventional obligations.*"[19] This conclusion was also forcefully defended by several dissenting judges in the Southwest Africa cases.[20] But for our purposes it is more important that the majority rejected that argument in the single international issue most appropriate for testing this doctrine. Unfortunately for the conviction that attaches to natural law approaches, general principles rarely point in one clear direction. Says Oscar Schachter:

Because principles are general and fundamental they tend to clash with each other in specific cases—thus every principle in the Charter can be paired off with a contrary or opposing principle in the context of a particular situation. . . . This characteristic opposition of principles is not, as some have suggested, the result of political confusion or defective drafting; on the contrary, *it is a desirable and necessary way of expressing the diverse and competing aims and interests of mankind.* An attempt to eliminate such inconsistencies can only result in an artificial emphasis on some abstractions and a suppression of valid and basic human values.[21]

But which is the valid and basic human value? Man's right to a fair trial or his right to have his local culture respected without outside interference? The very care taken by drafters to maintain the dualism Schachter so rightly emphasizes strongly suggests that everything remains squarely based on consent!

Aware of this dilemma, a group of outstanding legal scholars has attempted in recent years to provide a basis for the consistent development of universally shared values anchored in international law. Under the leadership of Professors Myres McDougal and Harold Lasswell, these scholars, sometimes dubbed the New Haven School, though not consciously working in the natural law tradition, are searching for general principles that could reconcile the self-interested conduct of governments with the needs of a universal world order. I suggest that this approach, in its determination to override the natural disposition of political actors to give expression only to *their* perceptions of their interests, approximates the concern of the natural lawyer. To obtain such a result, bases and doctrines other than the consent of the parties must necessarily be stressed.[22]

The authors of the New Haven School are all the more deserving of analysis in our context because they make a deliberate effort to link functional concerns and processes with the overarching objective of establishing a "world public order of human dignity." Functional needs are to be served by clarifying and anticipating major scientific and technological developments, as well as massive social transformations, and by assuming that these will in all likelihood lead to new inter-state conflicts. In order to avert or moderate such confrontations, the New Haven authors develop an intricate and sophisticated doctrine of treaty interpretation, designed to inspire confidence in the actors in international processes of regulation—in short, to create the intellectual and interest infrastructure for a stable world public order. Therefore "the goal is application of international agreements in terms of all community policies, including the policy of according the highest possible deference, compatible with other constitutional policies, to the genuine shared expectations of the particular parties."[23] When expectations are vague, they are to be reconciled in terms of the goals of public order; when expectations conflict with public order, they should not be given expression at all through judicial interpretation.

The nature of "world public order," then, becomes the key element, which provides a basis for interpreting the intentions of parties and even for overriding them. Specifically, the New Haven authors are explicit in arguing that the goals of human dignity should *always* override the expectations of particular parties. It is here that the natural law component enters. Human dignity is the most important, though not the sole, aspect of a world public order—a synonym, if you will, for the utopia cherished by authors. Since the notion of human dignity is not usually expressed in positive law, it is defined in terms of "basic community norms," a definition that appears to be very similar to the elusive general principles we discussed above. When developed in detail, the ideal of a world public order of human dignity becomes a world system in which all persons are given equal economic and educational opportunity, are allowed to participate in public decisions to the extent of their ability, are permitted to join voluntary organizations at will, are given the fullest possible political and social scope, and are protected against the arbitrary and excessive exercise of power, either by the state or by other groups or individuals—in effect a Great Society that covers the earth.

The difference between this approach and that of the ILO and the UN legal practitioners is in the slighting of the doctrine of consent by the New Haven authors. It is primarily judges and intellectuals in their public roles who are to work for the realization of this vision through interpretation, rather than treaty negotiators and their immediate clients, or international officials and their national opposite numbers. The merit of the approach is the simultaneous recognition of functional processes and ultimate values. Its weakness is the reliance on a set of base values—natural rights—that, in today's world, are parochial.

Not only does this approach reinforce the heavy incrustation of legal fictions that already characterizes the practice of treaty interpretation;[24] in its effort to free itself of the restraining doctrine of state consent, it reifies certain basic concepts that in turn command legitimacy only because of the supposed special knowledge of an elite group, alone capable of articulating ultimate values. If the members of that group all occupied equally powerful positions in the major world centers of influence and culture, a unified effort to place the achievement of human dignity above other objectives would certainly accelerate value sharing by way of international legal action. But the fact is that such a symmetrically placed elite does not exist.

CONCLUSION

And so we are condemned to the shoring up of basic human rights within the confining framework of divergent values and aspirations. To assert the reality of these forces is also to recognize that there is no escape—at the level of international action—from the doctrine of consent. This means that the international definition and protection of human rights will progress in certain regions favored by cultural and normative homogeneity, but not at the global level. It means that certain nations will continue to be very responsive to international influence, without implying any uniform and continuous UN role, evenly felt throughout the world. It certainly implies that opinion and policy will evolve more rapidly at the national and the regional levels than at Turtle Bay or the shores of Lac Léman. Some values will certainly be shared, but not to the point of realizing the universal aspirations of the great UN declarations. On the whole, for the next few decades values will continue to diverge, not merge at the point defined by the principles of these declarations.

But if they do not diverge too dramatically, it is still possible that, in the international system certain to follow the multi-bloc era we are now entering, a universal value scheme can develop out of a conjunction of national evolutionary patterns and international invocation. A functional strategy of fostering the institutionalization of human rights will then be vindicated, for it will have aided in creating clients, interests, norms, and expectations that can survive in a world of increasing divergence, to reassert their global potency at a time when mankind may—painfully— have learned a little more. In the absence of a stable, influential, and symmetrically distributed clientele, no natural law or universalist approach to human rights can claim as much. Thus what appears to be the second-best approach may yet turn out to be the best in the longer run of uneven human learning.

Methodological Appendix

Methodological Appendix

Judgments and classifications of the kind prominent in this study continue to be controversial. Nothing approaching certainty can be claimed for them, not only because of the unreliable character of many of the sources of data but because the very technique of establishing classifications requires explanation and justification. Hence I make no claim that the judgments and categories used here are equally applicable to other types of studies of state behavior in the context of international relations. The particular questions and hypotheses underlying each study must furnish the rationale for the appropriate categories and indicators.

The features of this study most in need of explanation—if they are to be accepted as throwing light on reality—are the periods into which the international system has been divided, the manner in which judgments on polity types have been made, the reliability of per capita energy consumption as an indicator of economic development, and the criteria used for determining prevailing economic institutions. Fortunately, two other scholars, Robert W. Cox and Harold K. Jacobson, are using similar criteria for classifying the world's nations in their study of decision-making in international organizations.[1] With their permission, I have checked their coding against mine with respect to polity types and economic development, and present the results here.

PERIODS AND THE INTERNATIONAL SYSTEM

By using the double criterion of the *distribution* and the *clustering* of state power in international relations, as described in Chapter 2,

I have divided the period since 1945 into five "historical systems," each with its own characteristic distribution of the aims of states, the methods employed, and the evolving tasks of international organizations.[2] Those systems are:

1945–47, Unipolar Victor Group. The victor nations in World War II in uneasy alliance, dictated the terms of world peace, and created the UN to serve their vision of the future. They wished to preserve the new political status quo and its frontiers, maintain the colonial system, and retain global free enterprise. The Soviet Union did not at that time openly challenge these aims. Collective security was to be maintained through Big Power consensus, the vanquished were to be forced to mend their undemocratic ways, and world trade and investment practices were to revert to free competition and private enterprise. Apart from collective security, the major tasks of international organizations were to be refugee relief and the restoration of non-discriminatory economic ties among nations.

1948–51, Tight Bipolar Symmetry. This is the era of the Cold War, with the world increasingly divided into a Western and a communist bloc. The West wished to preserve the status quo; the East wanted to expand into Europe and Asia by supporting nationalist and communist revolts. The West utilized bilateral economic aid and multilateral technical assistance to shore up its clients, and enlisted the UN collective security principle in its struggle with the East; the Soviets resisted these moves. Both sides made generous use of alliances, subversion, propaganda, and limited war. The protection of human rights as a UN concern originated in this period as part of the West's effort to discredit and embarrass Soviet practices.

1952–55, Loose Bipolar Heterosymmetry. In the wake of the Korean War, some Asian nations began to sound the theme of deliberate nonalignment with either bloc, a theme that reached its crescendo at the Bandung Conference. During this period the Western bloc continued to work for the preservation of the territorial status quo, but showed an increasing readiness to cater to various "third forces." The East continued to support nationalist and communist forces in revolt in Asia and Latin America. The Asian countries, and a few countries in Latin America and the Middle East, came to see in the Cold War an opportunity to gain concessions from both blocs to further their own national and economic development. The main blocs continued to build alliances, give bilateral military and economic aid, engage in propaganda and subversion, and intensify the nuclear arms race. The nonaligned countries increasingly engaged in active revolt and in agitation for decolonization and economic aid on a global scale. It was in this period that the first major UN responsibilities for economic and technical assistance were devised and the advocacy of internationally protected human rights gained force.

1956–60, Tripolar Heterosymmetry. The nonaligned countries tended more and more to act as a cohesive group with respect to economic development and decolonization, without, however, diminishing the military capability of the major blocs—though these blocs were less and less willing to make overt use of their might. The West sought to adapt to the changed circumstances by wooing the new group, or at least seeking to keep it neutral. The East responded in kind. The Third World, of course, profited from the competition, taking advantage of the situation to argue for further international means of spurring economic development through planning, more rapid decolonization, and more intensive protection of certain human rights, i.e., freedom from colonial rule and from racial discrimination. Multilateral economic aid evolved as a standard technique; peacekeeping under the auspices of small nations and of the UN Secretary-General became accepted; and the active intercession of the UN in forcing decolonization became a matter of routine. Both East and West went along with these trends, though both continued to intensify the bilateral arms race, practice propaganda, and support subversion. However, neither was now willing to engage the other in limited war, whereas the emerging new nations did so frequently, sometimes under the banner of self-determination.

1961–present, Multipolar Heterosymmetry, tending toward Asymmetry. The most recent period represents the culmination of the trends visible in 1960. The major alliances are losing cohesiveness. Soviet and American allies sometimes identify with the Third World. The balance of nuclear power has been stabilized to some extent through a series of arms control agreements. Decolonization has been virtually completed, thus giving the Third World almost a two-thirds majority in international councils. Multilateral economic aid and even planning is accepted as a technique by almost all nations, albeit with clear reluctance on the part of the United States and the Soviet Union. Propaganda and subversion are practiced less by the two super powers; military aid is given more selectively. Disenchantment with the results of intervention in the Third World is noticeable in both the United States and the Soviet Union. Limited war continues to be practiced by both against third countries. Third World countries engage in subversion, propaganda, and limited war against one another. There is a definite trend among these countries toward the formation of tight economic blocs in certain regions; similarly they show an increasing tendency to resist inclusion in a competitive and non-discriminatory world economy and to hold out instead for global planning for their benefit. However, they constitute a single bloc only for the purpose of advocating national self-determination, having broken into several blocs for most other purposes. Since these blocs are unequal in power and detract unevenly from the power of the major nations, the world system is increasingly asymmetrical.

CODING ECONOMIC INSTITUTIONS

Information for coding countries by economic institution was obtained from standard reference works, monographs on the economies of individual countries or regions, and informants I questioned on the subject. Each country was assessed on the basis of six characteristics: ownership of industry (public, private, or mixed); ownership of land (public, individual, or cooperative); extent of economic planning; fiscal measures for the control and distribution of income; legislation for the regulation of industrial and commercial practices; and extent of social welfare services. Capitalist, socialist, mixed, and corporatist economic systems would, ideally, look like the tabulation on the opposite page.

A word is necessary about corporatist institutions. They exist in very few countries, and combine private ownership of industry and agriculture with regulation in those areas via compulsory "corporations" of employers, workers, and government officials. These corporations sometimes also run the social services and impose rules governing competition among firms, investment practices, and labor relations. Corporatist institutions, seemingly a speciality of Mediterranean Europe and its offshoots (i.e., Brazil), have their root in certain Catholic social doctrines.

Characteristic	Capitalist	Socialist	Mixed	Corporatist
Ownership of industry	Overwhelmingly private	Overwhelmingly public	Largely private with a key public sector	Overwhelmingly private
Ownership of land	Overwhelmingly private	Public or collective	Private but with public services or subsidies	Overwhelmingly private
Economic planning	Absent or purely symbolic	Complete with production targets	Indicative, periodic forecasts, countercyclical policies	Either capitalist or mixed pattern
Fiscal measures	Absent or purely symbolic	Not necessary	Practiced regularly	Either capitalist or mixed pattern
Regulation of business	Rudimentary	Not necessary	Highly developed	Highly developed
Social services	Rudimentary	Highly developed	Highly developed	Desired in principle

Few countries meet all six requisites perfectly. I assigned countries to a given type if their institutions correspond to four or more of the typical attributes. A country with three attributes of a capitalist system and three of a socialist system was assigned to the mixed type.

COUNTRY CLASSIFICATIONS: POLITIES AND ECONOMIC DEVELOPMENT

Because of the importance of specific codings, I am presenting here the type of polity, the economic development category, and the economic institution to which I assigned each country during each of our five periods. My information on the attributes of regimes was obtained from monographs on individual countries and from standard reference works. Often this information had to be supplemented by informants, who were asked specific questions designed to throw light on the rather abstract regime categories "in action." These informants were always people with field experience in the country concerned. Among many, I should like to express here my gratitude especially to David E. Apter and Abdul A. Jalloh for help on the African countries, to Stuart Fagan for help on the Latin American states, to Clement Moore Henry and Sepehr Zabih for help on the Middle East, and to Chalmers Johnson, Daniel Lev, and Ralph Retzlaff for help on Asia.

Difficulties of course arose in instances where countries showed some attributes of one regime type and some of another. My final assignment was always made after long discussion with an informant familiar with the country, and after I had weighed the relative importance of each attribute in shaping the total polity. A judgment that had to be made fairly frequently was the distinction between a regime's *intention* to modernize, maintain the status quo, or change modestly, and its actual performance. The question was resolved in favor of intent, it being considered the more important variable in an enterprise seeking to pinpoint which human rights principles are likely to find application.

In the codings, which follow, I have used these abbreviations:

Regimes:

R	Reconciliation polity
M	Mobilization polity
A	Authoritarian polity
MA	Modernizing autocracy
TO	Traditional oligarchy
MO	Modernizing oligarchy
NC	Not classifiable
NI	Non-independent

Economic Development:

U	Underdeveloped
G	Growing
D	Developed
H	Highly developed

Economic Institutions:

C	Capitalist
S	Socialist
M	Mixed
CO	Corporatist
NC	Not classifiable

CLASSIFICATION OF STATES, 1945–47

State[a]	Haas coding			State	Haas coding		
	Regime	Economic development	Economic institutions		Regime	Economic development	Economic institutions
Afghanistan ...	TO	U	C	Ghana	NI	—	—
Albania	M	U	S	Greece	R	U	C
Algeria	NI	—	—	Guatemala	TO	U	C
Argentina	M	U	M	Guinea	NI	—	—
Australia	R	G	M	Guyana	NI	—	—
Austria	NI	—	—	Haiti	TO	U	C
Barbados	NI	—	—	Honduras	TO	U	C
Belgium	R	D	M	Hungary	M	U	S
Bolivia	TO	U	C	Iceland	R	G	M
Botswana	NI	—	—	India	NI	—	—
Brazil	A	U	CO	Indonesia	NI	—	—
Bulgaria	M	U	S	Iran	R	U	C
Burma	NI	—	—	Iraq	TO	U	C
Burundi	NI	—	—	Ireland	R	U	M
Cambodia	NI	—	—	Israel	NI	—	—
Cameroun	NI	—	—	Italy	R	U	M
Canada	R	D	M	Ivory Coast	NI	—	—
Central African				Jamaica	NI	—	—
Republic	NI	—	—	Japan	NI	—	—
Ceylon	NI	—	—	Jordan	NI	—	—
Chad	NI	—	—	Kenya	NI	—	—
Chile	R	U	C	Korea, Rep.	NI	—	—
China, Rep. ...	M	U	M	Kuwait	NI	—	—
Colombia	TO	U	C	Laos	NI	—	—
Congo (B)	NI	—	—	Lebanon	R	U	C
Congo (K)	NI	—	—	Lesotho	NI	—	—
Costa Rica	TO	U	C	Liberia	TO	U	C
Cuba	R	U	C	Libya	NI	—	—
Cyprus	NI	—	—	Luxembourg ...	R	D	M
Czechoslovakia	R	G	M	Malagasy Rep. ..	NI	—	—
Dahomey	NI	—	—	Malawi	NI	—	—
Denmark	R	G	M	Malaysia	NI	—	—
Dominican Rep.	TO	U	C	Maldives	NI	—	—
Ecuador	TO	U	C	Mali	NI	—	—
El Salvador	TO	U	C	Malta	NI	—	—
Ethiopia	MA	U	C	Mauritania	NI	—	—
Finland	R	U	M	Mexico	R	U	M
France	R	G	M	Morocco	NI	—	—
Gabon	NI	—	—	Nepal	NI	—	—
Gambia	NI	—	—	Netherlands ...	R	G	M
Germany, F.R.	NI	—	—	New Zealand ...	R	G	M

[a] Entities not coded because of the recent achievement of independence or autonomous status: Mauritius, Maldives, Nauru, Oman and Muscat, Swaziland, Dutch Antilles and Surinam, Associated States of the (British) West Indies, Trucial Coast states.

CLASSIFICATION OF STATES, 1945–47 (*cont'd*)

State	Haas coding			State	Haas coding		
	Regime	Economic development	Economic institutions		Regime	Economic development	Economic institutions
Nicaragua	TO	U	C	Thailand	MA	U	C
Niger	NI	—	—	Togo	NI	—	—
Nigeria	NI	—	—	Trinidad & Tob.	NI	—	—
Norway	R	D	M	Tunisia	NI	—	—
Outer Mongolia	M	U	S	Turkey	M	U	M
Pakistan	NI	—	—	Uganda	NI	—	—
Panama	TO	U	C	U.A.R.	TO	U	C
Paraguay	TO	U	C	U.K.	R	D	M
Peru	TO	U	C	U.S.S.R.	M	G	S
Philippines	R	U	C	U.S.	R	H	M
Poland	M	G	S	Upper Volta	NI	—	—
Portugal	A	U	CO	Uruguay	R	U	M
Romania	M	U	S	Venezuela	TO	U	C
Rwanda	NI	—	—	Vietnam, Rep.	NI	—	—
Saudi Arabia	TO	U	C	Yemen	TO	U	C
Senegal	NI	—	—	Yugoslavia	M	U	S
Sierra Leone	NI	—	—	Zambia	NI	—	—
Singapore	NI	—	—				
Somalia	NI	—	—	Entities of			
S. Africa	NC	G	C	uncertain status:			
S. Yemen	NI	—	—				
Spain	A	U	CO	China, P.R.	—	—	—
Sudan	NI	—	—	Germany, D.R.	NI	—	—
Swaziland	NI	—	—	Korea, P.R.	NI	—	—
Sweden	R	G	M	Bahrain	NI	—	—
Switzerland	R	G	M	Rhodesia	NI	—	—
Syria	TO	U	C	Vietnam, P.R.	NI	—	—
Tanzania	NI	—	—	W. Samoa	NI	—	—

CLASSIFICATION OF STATES, 1948–51

State	Haas coding			Cox-Jacobson coding	
	Regime	Economic development	Economic institutions	Regime	Economic development
Afghanistan	MA	U	C	A	U
Albania	M	U	S	M	U
Algeria	NI	—	—	NI	G
Argentina	M	U	M	M	G
Australia	R	D	M	R	H
Austria	R	G	M	NI	G
Barbados	NI	—	—	NI	G
Belgium	R	D	M	R	H
Bolivia	TO	U	C	A	U
Botswana	NI	—	—	NI	U
Brazil	R	U	CO	R	G
Bulgaria	M	U	S	M	U
Burma	R	U	C	R	U
Burundi	NI	—	—	NI	U
Cambodia	NI	—	—	A	U
Cameroun	NI	—	—	NI	U
Canada	R	H	M	R	H
Central African Republic ...	NI	—	—	NI	U
Ceylon	R	U	C	R	U
Chad	NI	—	—	NI	U
Chile	R	U	C	R	G
China, Rep.	M	U	M	A	U
Colombia	TO	U	C	A	G
Congo (B)	NI	—	—	NI	U
Congo (K)	NI	—	—	NI	U
Costa Rica	R	U	M	R	G
Cuba	R	U	C	R	G
Cyprus	NI	—	—	NI	G
Czechoslovakia	M	G	S	M	D
Dahomey	NI	—	—	NI	U
Denmark	R	G	M	R	H
Dominican Republic	TO	U	C	A	G
Ecuador	TO	U	C	A	U
El Salvador	TO	U	C	A	G
Ethiopia	MA	U	C	A	U
Finland	R	G	M	R	D
France	R	G	M	R	H
Gabon	NI	—	—	NI	U
Gambia	NI	—	—	NI	U
Germany, F.R.	R	G	M	R	D
Ghana	NI	—	—	NI	U
Greece	R	U	C	R	G
Guatemala	MO	U	C	M	U
Guinea	NI	—	—	NI	U
Guyana	NI	—	—	NI	U
Haiti	TO	U	C	A	U

CLASSIFICATION OF STATES, 1948–51 (*cont'd*)

State	Haas coding			Cox-Jacobson coding	
	Regime	Economic development	Economic institutions	Regime	Economic development
Honduras	TO	U	C	A	U
Hungary	M	U	S	M	G
Iceland	R	G	M	R	D
India	R	U	M	R	U
Indonesia	R	U	C	R	U
Iran	R	U	C	A	U
Iraq	TO	U	C	A	U
Ireland	R	G	M	R	G
Israel	R	U	M	R	G
Italy	R	U	M	R	G
Ivory Coast	NI	—	—	NI	U
Jamaica	NI	—	—	NI	U
Japan	R	U	C	R	G
Jordan	MA	U	C	A	U
Kenya	NI	—	—	NI	U
Korea, Rep.	A	U	C	A	U
Kuwait	NI	—	—	NI	H
Laos	NI	—	—	A	U
Lebanon	R	U	C	R	G
Lesotho	NI	—	—	NI	U
Liberia	TO	U	C	A	U
Libya	MA	U	C	NI	U
Luxembourg	R	D	M	R	H
Malagasy Rep.	NI	—	—	NI	U
Malawi	NI	—	—	NI	U
Malaysia	NI	—	—	NI	U
Mali	NI	—	—	NI	U
Malta	NI	—	—	NI	G
Mauritania	NI	—	—	NI	U
Mexico	R	U	M	R	G
Morocco	NI	—	—	NI	U
Nepal	MA	U	C	A	U
Netherlands	R	G	M	R	D
New Zealand	R	G	M	R	H
Nicaragua	TO	U	C	A	U
Niger	NI	—	—	NI	U
Nigeria	NI	—	—	NI	U
Norway	R	D	M	R	H
Outer Mongolia	M	U	S	M	U
Pakistan	R	U	M	A	U
Panama	TO	U	C	A	G
Paraguay	TO	U	C	A	U
Peru	TO	U	C	A	U
Philippines	R	U	C	R	G
Poland	M	G	S	M	G
Portugal	A	U	CO	A	G

CLASSIFICATION OF STATES, 1948–51 (*cont'd*)

State	Haas coding			Cox-Jacobson coding	
	Regime	Economic development	Economic institutions	Regime	Economic development
Romania	M	U	S	M	G
Rwanda	NI	—	—	NI	U
Saudi Arabia	TO	U	C	A	U
Senegal	NI	—	—	NI	U
Sierra Leone	NI	—	—	NI	U
Singapore	NI	—	—	NI	G
Somalia	NI	—	—	NI	U
South Africa	NC	G	C	A	G
South Yemen	NI	—	—	NI	U
Spain	A	U	CO	A	G
Sudan	NI	—	—	NI	U
Sweden	R	D	M	R	H
Switzerland	R	G	M	R	H
Syria	TO	U	C	A	U
Tanzania	NI	—	—	NI	U
Thailand	MA	U	C	A	U
Togo	NI	—	—	NI	U
Trinidad & Tobago	NI	—	—	NI	G
Tunisia	NI	—	—	NI	U
Turkey	R	U	M	R	G
Uganda	NI	—	—	NI	U
U.A.R.	TO	U	C	A	U
U.K.	R	D	M	R	H
U.S.S.R.	M	G	S	M	G
U.S.	R	H	M	R	H
Upper Volta	NI	—	—	NI	U
Uruguay	R	U	M	R	G
Venezuela	MO	U	C	A	D
Vietnam, Rep.	NI	—	—	NI	U
Yemen	TO	U	C	A	U
Yugoslavia	M	U	S	M	G
Zambia	NI	—	—	NI	U

Entities of uncertain status:

State	Regime	Economic development	Economic institutions	Regime	Economic development
China, P.R.	M	U	S	M	U
Germany, D.R.	M	G	S	M	G
Korea, P.R.	M	U	S	M	U
Bahrain	NI	—	—	NI	G
Rhodesia	NI	—	—	NI	U
Vietnam, P.R.	NI	—	—	NI	U
West Samoa	NI	—	—	NI	—

CLASSIFICATION OF STATES, 1952–55

State	Regime	Haas coding Economic development	Economic institutions	State	Regime	Haas coding Economic development	Economic institutions
Afghanistan ...	MA	U	C	Haiti	TO	U	C
Albania	M	U	S	Honduras	TO	U	C
Algeria	NI	—	—	Hungary	M	G	S
Argentina	M	U	M	Iceland	R	G	M
Australia	R	D	M	India	R	U	M
Austria	R	G	M	Indonesia	R	U	M
Barbados	NI	—	—	Iran	MA	U	C
Belgium	R	D	M	Iraq	TO	U	C
Bolivia	MO	U	M	Ireland	R	G	M
Botswana	NI	—	—	Israel	R	U	M
Brazil	R	U	M	Italy	R	U	M
Bulgaria	M	U	S	Ivory Coast	NI	—	—
Burma	A	U	C	Jamaica	NI	—	—
Burundi	NI	—	—	Japan	R	U	C
Cambodia	MA	U	C	Jordan	MO	U	C
Cameroun	NI	—	—	Kenya	NI	—	—
Canada	R	H	M	Korea, Rep.	A	U	C
Cent. African R.	NI	—	—	Kuwait	NI	—	—
Ceylon	R	U	M	Laos	TO	U	C
Chad	NI	—	—	Lebanon	R	U	C
Chile	R	U	C	Lesotho	NI	—	—
China, Rep. ...	M	U	M	Liberia	TO	U	C
Colombia	A	U	C	Libya	MA	U	C
Congo (B)	NI	—	—	Luxembourg ...	R	D	M
Congo (K)	NI	—	—	Malagasy Rep. .	NI	—	—
Costa Rica	R	U	M	Malawi	NI	—	—
Cuba	A	U	C	Malaysia	NI	—	—
Cyprus	NI	—	—	Maldives	NI	—	—
Czechoslovakia	M	D	S	Mali	NI	—	—
Dahomey	NI	—	—	Malta	NI	—	—
Denmark	R	G	M	Mauritania	NI	—	—
Dominican Rep.	TO	U	C	Mexico	R	U	M
Ecuador	TO	U	C	Morocco	NI	—	—
El Salvador	MO	U	C	Nepal	MA	U	C
Ethiopia	MA	U	C	Netherlands ...	R	G	M
Finland	R	G	M	New Zealand ...	R	G	M
France	R	G	M	Nicaragua	TO	U	C
Gabon	NI	—	—	Niger	NI	—	—
Gambia	NI	—	—	Nigeria	NI	—	—
Germany, F.R.	R	D	M	Norway	R	D	M
Ghana	NI	—	—	Outer Mongolia	M	U	S
Greece	R	U	C	Pakistan	R	U	M
Guatemala	M	U	M	Panama	TO	U	C
Guinea	NI	—	—	Paraguay	TO	U	C
Guyana	NI	—	—	Peru	MO	U	C

CLASSIFICATION OF STATES, 1952–55 (*cont'd*)

State	Haas coding			State	Haas coding		
	Regime	Economic development	Economic institutions		Regime	Economic development	Economic institutions
Philippines	R	U	C	Uganda	NI	—	—
Poland	M	G	S	U.A.R.	MO	U	M
Portugal	A	U	CO	U.K.	R	D	M
Romania	M	G	S	U.S.S.R.	M	G	S
Rwanda	NI	—	—	U.S.	R	H	M
Saudi Arabia ...	TO	U	C	Upper Volta ...	NI	—	—
Senegal	NI	—	—	Uruguay	R	U	M
Sierra Leone ...	NI	—	—	Venezuela	MO	G	C
Singapore	NI	—	—	Vietnam, Rep. .	MO	U	C
Somalia	NI	—	—	Yemen	TO	U	C
S. Africa	NC	G	C	Yugoslavia	M	U	S
S. Yemen	NI	—	—	Zambia	NI	—	—
Spain	A	U	CO				
Sudan	NI	—	—	Entities of			
Swaziland	NI	—	—	uncertain status:			
Sweden	R	D	M				
Switzerland	R	G	M	China, P.R.	M	U	S
Syria	TO	U	C	Germany, D.R. .	M	G	S
Tanzania	NI	—	—	Korea, P.R.	M	U	S
Thailand	MA	U	C	Bahrain	NI	—	—
Togo	NI	—	—	Rhodesia	NI	—	—
Trinidad & Tob.	NI	—	—	Vietnam, P.R. ..	M	U	S
Tunisia	NI	—	—	W. Samoa	NI	—	—
Turkey	R	U	M				

CLASSIFICATION OF STATES, 1956–60

State	Haas coding Regime	Economic development	Economic institutions	Cox-Jacobson coding Regime	Economic development
Afghanistan	MA	U	C	A	U
Albania	M	U	S	M	U
Algeria	NI	—	—	NI	G
Argentina	R	G	M	R	D
Australia	R	D	M	R	H
Austria	R	G	M	R	D
Barbados	NI	—	—	NI	G
Belgium	R	D	M	R	H
Bolivia	MO	U	M	M	U
Botswana	NI	—	—	NI	U
Brazil	R	U	M	R	G
Bulgaria	M	G	S	M	G
Burma	MO	U	M	R	U
Burundi	NI	—	—	NI	U
Cambodia	MA	U	C	A	U
Cameroun	A	U	C	NI	U
Canada	R	D	M	R	H
Central African Republic	A	U	C	NI	U
Ceylon	R	U	M	R	U
Chad	A	U	C	NI	U
Chile	R	U	M	R	G
China, Rep.	M	U	M	A	U
Colombia	R	U	C	R	G
Congo (B)	MA	U	C	NI	U
Congo (K)	NI	—	—	NI	U
Costa Rica	R	U	M	R	G
Cuba	A	U	C	A	G
Cyprus	NI	—	—	NI	G
Czechoslovakia	M	D	S	M	D
Dahomey	R	U	C	NI	U
Denmark	R	G	M	R	H
Dominican Republic	TO	U	C	A	G
Ecuador	TO	U	C	A	G
El Salvador	MO	U	C	A	G
Ethiopia	MA	U	C	A	U
Finland	R	G	M	R	D
France	R	G	M	R	H
Gabon	MA	U	C	NI	G
Gambia	NI	—	—	NI	U
Germany, F.R.	R	D	M	R	D
Ghana	M	U	S	M	U
Greece	R	U	C	R	G
Guatemala	A	U	C	A	G
Guinea	M	U	S	M	U
Guyana	M	—	—	NI	G
Haiti	TO	U	C	A	U

CLASSIFICATION OF STATES, 1956–60 (*cont'd*)

State	Haas coding			Cox-Jacobson coding	
	Regime	Economic development	Economic institutions	Regime	Economic development
Honduras	A	U	C	A	G
Hungary	M	G	S	M	G
Iceland	R	D	M	R	H
India	R	U	M	R	U
Indonesia	M	U	S	M	U
Iran	MA	U	C	A	U
Iraq	M	U	M	M	G
Ireland	R	G	M	R	D
Israel	R	G	M	R	D
Italy	R	U	M	R	D
Ivory Coast	A	U	M	NI	U
Jamaica	NI	—	—	NI	G
Japan	R	U	C	R	G
Jordan	MO	U	C	A	U
Kenya	NI	—	—	NI	U
Korea, Rep.	A	U	M	A	U
Kuwait	NI	—	—	NI	H
Laos	TO	U	C	A	U
Lebanon	R	U	C	A	G
Lesotho	NI	—	—	NI	U
Liberia	A	U	C	A	U
Libya	MA	U	C	A	U
Luxembourg	R	D	M	R	H
Malagasy Rep.	A	U	C	NI	U
Malawi	NI	—	—	NI	U
Malaysia	R	U	C	R	G
Mali	M	U	S	NI	U
Malta	NI	—	—	NI	G
Mauritania	NI	—	—	NI	U
Mexico	R	U	M	R	G
Morocco	MA	U	C	A	U
Nepal	MA	U	C	A	U
Netherlands	R	G	M	R	D
New Zealand	R	G	M	R	H
Nicaragua	MO	U	C	A	G
Niger	A	U	C	NI	U
Nigeria	R	U	C	NI	U
Norway	R	G	M	R	H
Outer Mongolia	M	U	S	M	U
Pakistan	A	U	M	A	U
Panama	TO	U	C	A	G
Paraguay	TO	U	C	A	U
Peru	R	U	C	R	G
Philippines	R	U	C	R	G
Poland	M	G	S	M	G
Portugal	A	U	CO	A	G

CLASSIFICATION OF STATES, 1956–60 (*cont'd*)

State	Haas coding			Cox-Jacobson coding	
	Regime	Economic development	Economic institutions	Regime	Economic development
Romania	M	G	S	M	G
Rwanda	NI	—	—	NI	U
Saudi Arabia	TO	U	C	A	G
Senegal	A	U	C	NI	U
Sierra Leone	NI	—	—	NI	U
Singapore	NI	—	—	NI	G
Somalia	NI	—	—	NI	U
South Africa	NC	G	C	A	G
South Yemen	NI	—	—	NI	U
Spain	A	U	CO	A	G
Sudan	MO	U	M	A	U
Sweden	R	D	M	R	H
Switzerland	R	G	M	R	H
Syria	M	U	M	NI	U
Tanzania	NI	—	—	NI	U
Thailand	MA	U	C	A	U
Togo	A	U	C	NI	U
Trinidad & Tobago	NI	—	—	NI	G
Tunisia	A	U	M	A	U
Turkey	A	U	M	R	G
Uganda	NI	—	—	NI	U
U.A.R.	M	U	S	M	U
U.K.	R	D	M	R	H
U.S.S.R.	M	G	S	M	D
U.S.	R	H	M	R	H
Upper Volta	A	U	C	NI	U
Uruguay	R	U	M	R	G
Venezuela	R	G	M	R	D
Vietnam, Rep.	A	U	CO	A	U
Yemen	TO	U	C	A	U
Yugoslavia	M	U	S	M	G
Zambia	NI	—	—	NI	U
Entities of uncertain status:					
China, P.R.	M	U	S	M	U
Germany, D.R.	M	D	S	M	D
Korea, P.R.	M	U	S	M	U
Bahrain	NI	—	—	NI	G
Rhodesia	NI	—	—	NI	U
Vietnam, P.R.	M	U	S	M	U
West Samoa	NI	—	—	NI	—

CLASSIFICATION OF STATES, 1961–68

State	Haas coding			Cox-Jacobson coding	
	Regime	Economic development	Economic institutions	Regime	Economic development
Afghanistan	MA	U	C	A	U
Albania	M	U	S	M	U
Algeria	M	U	S	M	G
Argentina	A	G	M	A	D
Australia	R	D	M	R	H
Austria	R	G	M	R	H
Barbados	R	U	C	R	G
Belgium	R	D	M	R	H
Bolivia	A	U	M	A	U
Botswana	MA	U	C	A	U
Brazil	A	U	M	A	G
Bulgaria	M	G	S	M	G
Burma	MO	U	S	A	U
Burundi	TO	U	C	A	U
Cambodia	MA	U	M	A	U
Cameroun	A	U	C	A	U
Canada	R	H	M	R	H
Central African Republic ...	A	U	C	A	U
Ceylon	R	U	M	R	U
Chad	A	U	C	A	U
Chile	R	G	M	R	D
China, Rep.	M	U	M	A	G
Colombia	R	U	M	R	G
Congo (B)	M	U	C	M	U
Congo (K)	A	U	C	A	U
Costa Rica	R	U	M	R	G
Cuba	M	U	S	M	G
Cyprus	R	U	M	A	D
Czechoslovakia	M	D	S	M	D
Dahomey	A	U	C	A	U
Denmark	R	D	M	R	H
Dominican Republic	R	U	C	R	G
Ecuador	TO	U	C	R	G
El Salvador	MO	U	C	A	G
Ethiopia	MA	U	C	A	U
Finland	R	G	M	R	H
France	R	G	M	R	H
Gabon	MA	U	C	A	G
Gambia	R	U	C	R	U
Germany, F.R.	R	D	M	R	H
Ghana	A	U	S	A	G
Greece	R	U	C	A	D
Guatemala	A	U	C	A	G
Guinea	M	U	S	M	U
Guyana	R	U	C	R	G
Haiti	TO	U	C	A	U

CLASSIFICATION OF STATES, 1961–68 (*cont'd*)

State	Haas coding			Cox-Jacobson coding	
	Regime	Economic development	Economic institutions	Regime	Economic development
Honduras	A	U	C	A	G
Hungary	M	G	S	M	D
Iceland	R	D	M	R	H
India	R	U	M	R	U
Indonesia	M	U	S	A	U
Iran	MA	U	C	A	G
Iraq	M	U	M	M	G
Ireland	R	G	M	R	D
Israel	R	G	M	R	D
Italy	R	G	M	R	H
Ivory Coast	A	U	M	A	G
Jamaica	R	U	C	R	G
Japan	R	G	C	R	D
Jordan	MO	U	C	A	G
Kenya	A	U	M	A	U
Korea, Rep.	A	U	M	A	U
Kuwait	MA	U	C	A	H
Laos	TO	U	C	A	U
Lebanon	R	U	C	R	G
Lesotho	MA	U	C	A	U
Liberia	A	U	C	A	G
Libya	MA	U	C	A	D
Luxembourg	R	D	M	R	H
Malagasy Rep.	A	U	C	A	U
Malawi	A	U	C	A	U
Malaysia	R	U	C	R	G
Mali	M	U	S	M	U
Malta	R	U	M	R	G
Mauritania	M	U	C	A	U
Mexico	R	U	M	R	G
Morocco	MA	U	C	A	G
Nepal	MA	U	C	A	U
Netherlands	R	D	M	R	H
New Zealand	R	G	M	R	H
Nicaragua	MO	U	C	A	G
Niger	A	U	C	A	U
Nigeria	R	U	C	A	U
Norway	R	D	M	R	H
Outer Mongolia	M	U	S	M	U
Pakistan	A	U	M	A	U
Panama	TO	U	C	A	G
Paraguay	TO	U	C	A	G
Peru	R	U	C	R	G
Philippines	R	U	C	R	G
Poland	M	D	S	M	D
Portugal	A	U	CO	A	G

CLASSIFICATION OF STATES, 1961–68 (*cont'd*)

State	Haas coding			Cox-Jacobson coding	
	Regime	Economic development	Economic institutions	Regime	Economic development
Romania	M	G	S	M	G
Rwanda	MO	U	C	A	U
Saudi Arabia	TO	U	C	A	G
Senegal	A	U	C	A	U
Sierra Leone	R	U	C	A	U
Singapore	R	U	C	R	G
Somalia	M	U	C	A	U
South Africa	NC	G	C	A	G
South Yemen	M	U	?	M	U
Spain	A	U	M	A	D
Sudan	A	U	M	A	U
Sweden	R	D	M	R	H
Switzerland	R	G	M	R	H
Syria	M	U	S	M	U
Tanzania	M	U	M	M	U
Thailand	MA	U	C	A	U
Togo	A	U	C	A	U
Trinidad & Tobago	R	G	C	R	D
Tunisia	A	U	S	M	G
Turkey	MO	U	M	R	G
Uganda	A	U	C	M	U
U.A.R.	M	U	S	M	U
U.K.	R	D	M	R	H
U.S.S.R.	M	D	S	M	D
U.S.	R	H	M	R	H
Upper Volta	A	U	C	A	U
Uruguay	R	U	M	R	D
Venezuela	R	G	M	R	D
Vietnam Rep.	A	U	NC	A	U
Yemen	M	U	C	A	U
Yugoslavia	M	G	S	M	G
Zambia	A	U	C	M	G
Entities of uncertain status:					
China, P.R.	M	U	S	M	U
Germany, D.R.	M	D	S	M	H
Korea, P.R.	M	U	S	M	U
Bahrain	TO	U	C	NI	U
Rhodesia	NC	U	C	A	U
Vietnam, P.R.	M	U	S	M	U
West Samoa	TO	U	M	—	—

INTER-CODER COMPARISON: REGIME TYPES

As Table A.1 shows, the agreement among the two sets of coders is excellent. Disagreement on grounds of different factual estimations is limited to 5.4 per cent of the items coded. Another 6.3 per cent involved disagreement because of different methods used in pinpointing the time of the determination. Cox and Jacobson made their determination in specific years, 1950, 1958, and 1967. I made my determination by examining regime characteristics over a period of years, e.g., 1948–51 or 1961–68, and coding on the basis of the characteristics that prevailed during at least half of the period. In instances of regime change within a period, my method fails to capture the type that was in power less than half the time. The largest discrepancy on grounds of time occurred because the two sets of coders did not use identical criteria for deciding when the former French African colonies attained independence, i.e., 1958 as opposed to 1960.

It should be noted, of course, that Cox and Jacobson used three regime types, whereas I used six. They considered every polity that was neither clearly competitive nor clearly mobilization-oriented authoritarian. I broke non-reconciliation and non-mobilization regimes into four types: modernizing autocracies, modernizing oligarchies, traditional oligarchies, and authoritarian polities. My definitions and operational criteria are presented in Chapter 2. Cox and Jacobson characterize a competitive (reconciliation) regime as one having two or more political parties and other autonomous organizations that legally compete with each other for influence and freely elect the government; these groups stand a good chance

TABLE A.1

Inter-Coder Comparison: Regime Types
(per cent)

		Disagree	
Total items	Agree	Timing reasons	Substantive reasons[a]
100.0	88.3	6.3	5.4
(392)	(346)	(25)	(21)

[a] Countries coded differently for substantive reasons: China (Taiwan), South Africa, Rhodesia, Iran (1950), Pakistan (1950), Burma (1958), Bolivia (1958), Turkey (1958), Cyprus (1967), Ecuador (1967), Indonesia (1967), Mauritania (1967), Somalia (1967), Tunisia (1967), Uganda (1967), Yemen (1967), Zambia (1967).

of having their way. They define mobilization regimes essentially as I do and authoritarian regimes as encompassing the four types listed above.[3] Both sets of coders agreed that no single criterion can determine a classification, and that all criteria must be used and evaluated jointly in order to capture the true character of a regime. Moreover, consultations took place between the two sets of coders to discuss the application of criteria to specific cases.

But, despite consultations and a broad consensus on criteria, one persistent difference of opinion remains: it is still difficult in some cases to distinguish a mobilization regime from a looser kind of authoritarianism. I regard Taiwan, Somalia, Mauritania, and Yemen (under the Egyptian-sponsored government) as mobilization regimes in intent, if not in day-to-day conduct; Cox and Jacobson consider them merely authoritarian. But they consider Tunisia, Uganda, and Zambia mobilization regimes, whereas I coded them as authoritarian. Clearly, none of these cases is unambiguous, and I admit that both Tunisia and Zambia have certain features of a mobilization regime—but not enough in my judgment to so code them. Differences of this kind cannot be resolved until we all agree on a standard list of criteria more discriminating than the ones we are presently employing.

INTER-CODER COMPARISON: ECONOMIC DEVELOPMENT

Differences in judgment are far more pronounced when we come to the indicators of economic development. As Table A.2 shows, complete agreement was obtained on only half of the items coded. Both sets of coders used a four-point scale; mine was based on per capita energy consumption, the Cox-Jacobson scale on per capita GNP. I explained my preference for the indicator of per

TABLE A.2

Inter-Coder Comparison: Economic Development
(per cent)

Total items	Agree	Cox-Jacobson rate higher by:		
		1 point	2 points[a]	3 points
100.0	50.5	41.9	7.6	Negligible
(315)	(159)	(132)	(23)	(Kuwait only)

[a] Countries rated 2 points higher: Denmark, France, New Zealand, Switzerland, Venezuela, Iceland, Italy, Norway, Austria, Cyprus, Finland, Greece, Libya, Spain, Uruguay.

capita energy consumption in Chapter 2; the justification is specific to the objective at hand: to rank countries on the basis of the welfare of the working population likely to join trade unions. As will become apparent, there are systematic differences in classification, depending on which indicator is used; neither can be considered uniquely reliable or useful. The two scales are as follows:

Type of country[a]	Per capita energy consumption[b]	Per capita GNP[c]
Underdeveloped	0 to .99	0 to 199
Growing	1 to 2.99	200 to 599
Developed	3 to 5.99	600 to 999
Highly developed	Over 6	Over 1000

[a] The labels attached to each type are mine alone. The descriptions of the corresponding types used by Cox and Jacobson appear on p. 50 of their manuscript.

[b] In metric tons of coal equivalent per annum. The coding was based on the mean figure for the period of years encompassed in a given range, e.g., 1952–55 or 1961–68, as reported in UN *Statistical Yearbook.*

[c] In U.S. dollars at 1965 prices, for 1953, 1958, and 1965, as reported in UN *Yearbook of National Accounts Statistics*, and UN *Statistical Yearbook.* For assumptions about and special interpretations of this data, see Cox and Jacobson, "Decision-Making in International Organizations: An Interim Report" (paper delivered at the 65th Annual Meeting of the American Political Science Association, New York, September 1969), pp. 50–51. (Mimeo.)

First we must try to pinpoint the reasons for discrepancies of only one point on the scale. In *all* cases of divergence, the per capita GNP ratings place a country on a higher point of the scale than the per capita energy ratings. Moreover, this trend is uniformly true for all points on the scale. In short, countries that are placed at the top of the underdeveloped, growing, and developed categories according to energy consumption appear at the bottom of the next highest category when classified according to GNP. This trend persists, despite the fact that our energy ratings are based on a mean figure covering several years and the GNP ratings are based on single years.

Who is right and who is wrong? It all depends on what the indicator is supposed to indicate. I am satisfied that if we wish to focus on the welfare of the lower strata of a society, we are better off using an indicator that exaggerates low living standards; on the other hand, if we wish to stress capital available for investment or industrialization, it makes sense to slur over intra-national differences in income and focus on the aggregate income.

This rationale, however, is inadequate for dealing with cases of discrepancy involving two points on the scale, 7.6 per cent of the items coded. Why should I rank Greece, Libya, and Spain as "underdeveloped" and Cox and Jacobson rank them as "developed"? Why should France, New Zealand, Iceland, and Venezuela appear as "growing" on my scale, but as "highly developed" on theirs? Again, part of the answer lies in the selection of the year used for the rankings. An average for the period 1961–68 will yield a slightly lower score than that arrived at when the year 1965 is used, at least in Western Europe. I am nevertheless persuaded that the energy consumption index seriously *understates* levels of economic development in certain industrial nations, as judged by such ancillary indicators of well-being as literacy, tourism, and the availability of urban comforts for the overwhelming portion of the population. Hence the following countries, at least during the most recent period, should be moved up one category from the one in which the energy consumption index places them: Denmark, France, New Zealand, Switzerland, Iceland, Italy, Norway, Austria, Finland, and Uruguay. It is for this reason that most of my tabulations in the text group together developed and growing reconciliation policies.

On the other hand, it seems to me that the following countries are given an exaggerated ranking on the GNP index, if the situation is read jointly with the ancillary indicators of well-being, and should therefore be moved down one category: Cyprus, Greece, Libya, Spain, Venezuela (before 1961), and Kuwait. Since Greece, Libya, Spain, and Venezuela occupy important historical positions in the evolution of the ILO system of protecting trade union rights, our findings must be read in the context of some uncertainty about their true degree of economic underdevelopment.

Notes

1. Proclamation of Teheran, Articles 1, 2, and 11, *United Nations Monthly Chronicle* (June 1968), pp. 91–103.

2. Among the suggestions for such machinery not considered at Teheran but forwarded to the UN, we find proposals for the creation of new international judicial organs, for the improvement of the triennial reporting system, for the institution of a committee to expedite the ratification of international human rights conventions, and for the establishment of national human rights commissions.

3. For an excellent argument suggesting the superficial character of the global integration process, see Michael Barkun, "Integration, Organization, and Values," in Robert W. Gregg and Michael Barkun, eds., *The United Nations System and Its Functions* (Princeton, N.J.: Van Nostrand, 1968), pp. 458–60.

4. Frederick van Asbeck, "Growth and Movement in International Law," *International and Comparative Law Quarterly*, Vol. XI (1962), 1072. Van Asbeck had many decades of experience in supervising the implementation of human rights conventions both in the League of Nations and the ILO.

5. Myres S. McDougal, Harold D. Lasswell, and W. Michael Reisman, "Theories about International Law: Prologue to a Configurative Jurisprudence," *Virginia Journal of International Law*, VIII, 2 (April 1968), 298.

6. René Cassin, representing France at the UNESCO General Conference session adopting the convention, complained of this feature, as did Suzanne Bastid in "Une Nouvelle Commission de Conciliation," *Mélanges Offerts à Henri Rolin* (Paris: Pedone, 1964), pp. 1–12. Mme. Bastid, however, never once referred to the approach of the ILO, which comes close to her objective. Similarly, Sandifer and Scheman, in their effort to perfect the Inter-American Committee on Human Rights so as to make it acces-

sible to the individual without falling afoul of the intervention argument, ignore the successful experience of the ILO in overcoming this legal objection. Durward V. Sandifer and L. Ronald Scheman, *The Foundations of Freedom: the Interrelationship Between Democracy and Human Rights* (New York: Praeger, 1966).

7. Egon Schwelb, "Human Rights," *Annual Review of United Nations Affairs, 1962–63*, pp. 115–16.

8. Myres S. McDougal and Gerhard Bebr, "Human Rights in the United Nations," *American Journal of International Law*, LVIII, 3 (July 1964), 639.

9. Rosalyn Higgins, *The Development of International Law Through the Political Organs of the United Nations* (London: Oxford University Press, 1963), pp. 118–30; Hersch Lauterpacht, *International Law and Human Rights* (New York: Praeger, 1950). Hans Kelsen, incidentally, came to the opposite conclusion: Articles 55 and 56 did not create any new legal obligations. See his *Law of the United Nations* (London: Stevens, 1950), pp. 29, 33. See also the comprehensive discussion of the learned but inconclusive legal debate in Manouchehr Ganji, *International Protection of Human Rights* (Geneva: Droz, 1962), pp. 116–19.

10. Ganji, pp. 167–227.

11. Richard B. Bilder, "The International Promotion of Human Rights: A Current Assessment," *American Journal of International Law*, LVIII, 3 (July 1964), 732. See also by the same author "Rethinking International Human Rights: Some Basic Questions," *Wisconsin Law Review*, 1969, 1, pp. 171–217, for a painstaking and unflinching examination of the logic underlying the purely legal-constitutional advocacy of the human rights cause, which arrives at conclusions basically similar to mine with respect to the virtues of a more indirect and less self-righteous approach. For similar conclusions, see S. P. Sharma, "The Promotion of International Protection of Human Rights," *International Studies* (New Delhi), special issue, October 1965.

12. The functional logic as a way of linking organizational programs with value change is described in detail in my *Beyond the Nation-State* (Stanford, Calif.: Stanford University Press, 1964), Chapters 2, 13, 14.

13. Rita F. and Howard J. Taubenfeld, *Race, Peace, Law and Southern Africa* (working paper, the Hammarskjöld Forums. New York: Association of the Bar of the City of New York, 1966), p. 44.

14. Dag Hammarskjöld, *Servant of Peace* (London: Bodley Head, 1962), p. 134.

15. C. Wilfred Jenks, *Law in the World Community* (New York: David McKay, 1967), p. 158. Paradoxically, Jenks concludes this passage by arguing that "therein lies the case for the acceptance of international obligations in respect of human rights by all who believe that their own record

in respect of human rights defies comparison." If my hands are clean would I submit my case to a panel of judges whose hands I consider sullied? While admitting the fact of cultural and political diversity, Jenks tries to use that as an additional argument for encouraging the sharing of norms.

16. David Mitrany has summarized this trend briefly. See the discussion on human rights at the International Political Science Association Conference, Geneva, September 1964. (Mimeo.)

17. For a sensitive discussion of these violations, stressing personal liberty, freedom of the press, and the suppression of political parties, see David H. Bailey, *Public Liberties in the New States* (Chicago: Rand, McNally, 1964). Ali Mazrui demonstrates that for many African nations the issue of human rights has priority over the maintenance of peace and security as a purpose of the UN ("The United Nations and some African Political Attitudes," in Gregg and Barkun, pp. 47–51). But since to them the "protection" of human rights means essentially the punishment of South Africa and Portugal, and the elimination of *apartheid* and other forms of racial discrimination (China's threat to Tibet, for instance, was largely a matter of indifference), we can say that the African concern for human rights is the equivalent of militant anti-racism and anti-colonialism, not a sentiment favoring individual freedom.

18. For details on this argument, see Haas, *Beyond the Nation-State*, Chapters 8, 11.

19. Oscar Schachter sketches much the same kind of approach toward determining the nature of legal obligation in a world legal order filled with new kinds of demands and client groups. See his "Towards a Theory of International Obligation," *Virginia Journal of International Law*, VIII, 2 (April 1968), especially pp. 314–19.

20. For details, see "Issues Before the 23rd General Assembly," *International Conciliation*, No. 569 (September 1968), pp. 93–98.

21. Such a purpose is not achieved, however, by simple and unstinting praise or admiration, particularly if the praise is based simply on paper procedures and ratification statistics! For an example of uncritical admiration, see W. Paul Gormley, "The Emerging Protection of Human Rights by the International Labor Organization," *Albany Law Review*, XXX (1966), 13–51.

CHAPTER TWO

1. The only full-scale study of this committee and the supervisory system in general is E. A. Landy, *The Effectiveness of International Supervision: Thirty Years of I.L.O. Experience* (London: Stevens, 1966).

2. For the text of these and other ILO conventions, see ILO, *Interna-*

tional Labour Code (Geneva, 1951). For an authoritative and extensive discussion, see C. Wilfred Jenks, *The International Protection of Trade Union Freedom* (London: Stevens, 1957), pp. 24–31.

3. See Haas, *Beyond the Nation-State*, pp. 355–70, for an analysis of all the cases and the procedure.

4. See *ibid.*, pp. 352–54, 381–83, for the details on the origin of the machinery.

5. Further details on the periodization of the international system are provided in the Methodological Appendix, pp. 137–59.

6. For full tabulations on the regime categories to which countries were assigned, see *ibid.*, pp. 143–55. Economic development categories are also discussed more fully in the appendix as are methods of coding for economic institutions. The regime categories are adapted from David E. Apter, *The Politics of Modernization* (Chicago: University of Chicago Press, 1965), notably Chapters 10, 11.

CHAPTER THREE

1. Thus acceptance is calculated by the formula

$$\frac{\text{actual ratifications}}{\text{possible ratifications}}$$

Actual ratifications were taken from ILO, "International Labour Conventions: Chart of Ratifications" (Geneva, June 1, 1964). Possible ratifications were computed by taking the total of the conventions studied by E. A. Landy (*Effectiveness of International Supervision*) and correcting it for non-applicability or irrelevance to certain member nations. Thus states without a seacoast were not debited with maritime conventions and texts dealing with fishermen; many underdeveloped nations with scant prospects of using nuclear reactors were not debited with the convention dealing with radiation hazards. Declarations of acceptance deposited by colonial powers with respect to their non-metropolitan territories were not counted. Possible scores range from 1 to 0.

It may be objected that a state's failure to ratify a text does not in itself prove that the state rejects the values implicit in the convention; nations may decline to ratify for a number of technical reasons (e.g., federations or countries that do not possess the administrative machinery to make a text meaningful) and still subscribe to the norms. This objection is valid. Our measure, therefore, records only the unwillingness of states—for whatever reason—to subscribe to the supervisory procedure associated with these texts. It records their unwillingness to report regularly, to submit to collective scrutiny, to provide explanations, and to subject themselves to such possible international sanctions as blacklisting or a visit from a commission of inquiry. It does not, however, measure directly their rejection of the norms themselves.

2. Landy, pp. 68–69. Conformity is calculated by the formula

$$1 - \frac{\text{critical observations}}{\text{actual ratifications}}$$

Landy's figures include data on non-metropolitan territories, which have been excluded from these tabulations, thus accounting for the slight difference between his figures and ours. Possible scores range from 1 to $-\infty$.

3. Implementation is calculated by the formula

$$\frac{\text{action in full} + .5 \ (\text{action in part})}{\text{critical observations}}$$

Landy, pp. 217, 255, provided the data for these computations. Figures for non-metropolitan territories were omitted. Landy's definitions of "action in full" and "action in part" were accepted. Possible scores range from 1 to 0.

4. A comparison of scores on ILO and UN human rights conventions is shown in the tabulation on p. 166. Data for the 1968 membership of the UN Commission on Human Rights are based on acceptance scores for 16 UN human rights conventions, as reported in UN doc. A/CONF. 32/15, 28 March 1968.

CHAPTER FOUR

1. Case 10 (Chile, 1951); Case 121 (Greece, 1955). Many of the complaints brought against the U.S. were actually charges advanced jointly against the U.S. and Greece by exiled Greek unions affiliated with the WFTU. They were coded against the U.S. in this study and treated as Cold War–connected.

2. The best known cases include Nos. 14 (Czechoslovakia, 1951), 19 (Hungary, 1952), 58 (Poland, 1952), 111 (U.S.S.R., 1950–54), 148 (Poland, 1956), 155 (U.S.S.R., 1956), 158 (Hungary, 1956), and 160 (Hungary, 1957). The last four cases were brought in response to the events in Hungary and Poland in 1956 and the Soviet military intervention. Other convictions in this category include a number of adverse judgments brought against Castro's Cuba in the mid-1960s.

3. Case 194 (1959–68).

4. Case 156 (1956–63). The case became moot with the French withdrawal from Algeria.

5. The most spectacular cases are No. 152 (Northern Rhodesia, 1956–59) and Nos. 221 and 291 (Aden, 1962–66). The Aden cases became moot with the independence of South Yemen. Though Britain never implemented the ILO decisions there, she did carry out the recommendations in favor of African unions in Northern Rhodesia.

6. Cases 102, 200, 261, 300, 314 (1954–63). Other convictions of South Africa were in a more restricted trade union issue context.

Tabulation for Note 4, Chapter 3

Country	All ILO Conventions			ILO Human Rights Conventions			UN Human Rights Conventions
	Accept	Conform	Implement	Accept	Conform	Implement	Accept
Argentina	.60	.35	.30	.86	1.00		.43
Austria	.46	.48	.72	.86	.83	.00	.25
Chile	.39	.40	.45	.29	.50	.00	.12
Dahomey	.16	.93	.50	.71	.80	.50	.12
France	.65	.62	.54	.71	.60	1.00	.50
Greece	.32	.31	.50	.71	.80	.50	.25
Guatemala	.17	.19	.23	.71	.60	.25	.25
India	.26	.36	.69	.57	.75	.00	.31
Iran	.03	1.00		.29	1.00		.18
Israel	.29	.54	.63	.71	.20	.00	.50
Italy	.58	.64	.57	.86	.83	.50	.31
Jamaica	.18	1.00		.71	1.00		.37
Malagasy Republic	.16	.73	.25	.71	.20	.00	.18
Morocco	.26	.60	.50	.57	.75	.50	.25
New Zealand	.42	.81	.63	.29	1.00		.31
Nigeria	.19	.94	.00	.71	1.00		.25
Pakistan	.27	.76	.17	.86	.67	.25	.37
Peru	.16	.50	.25	.86	.67	.00	.12
Philippines	.16	.53	.07	.71	.60	.00	.43
Poland	.52	.62	.50	1.00	.43	.00	.37
Senegal	.23	.95	.00	.86	.83	.00	.18
Sweden	.29	.62	.45	1.00	.86	.00	.55
Tanzania	.25	1.00		.57	1.00		.25
U.S.S.R.	.23	.73	.25	.86	.33	.13	.37
U.A.R.	.31	.67	.45	1.00	.57	.33	.37
U.S.	.04	1.00		.00			.18
Venezuela	.19	.50	.28	.29	−1.00	.00	.18
Yugoslavia	.49	.52	.71	.86	1.00		.68

Lebanon and the Ukrainian S.S.R., both members of the commission, were not tabulated in the ILO data.

7. Cases 103 (1954), 251 (1961), 298 (1963–65). In Case 414 (1965–68) the same charges were being pressed against independent Rhodesia.

8. Cases 266 (Portugal, 1962) and 143 (Spain, 1956).

9. Cases 294, 383, 397, 400, 497, 520 (1962–68). All of these cases were consolidated by the ILO committee into one massive indictment of the

Spanish system before an agreement was reached in 1968 permitting the dispatch of a fact-finding committee to Spain.

10. Cases 282, 401 (Burundi, 1962, 1964) ; Case 168 (Paraguay, 1960).

11. Case 202 (Thailand, 1959–68) ; Case 274 (Libya, 1962–68).

12. Case 506 (1967).

13. Case 303 (1963–65).

14. Cases 185, 224, 234, 256, 464, 481, 517, 519 (1958–68). Most of these cases were consolidated by the ILO committee into one massive case after the military dictatorship was established in April 1967. Earlier, in 1965, an agreement was reached, whereby the Fact-Finding and Conciliation Commission was to be sent to Greece in an effort to clear up the post–civil war situation.

15. Cases 191 (Sudan under the Abboud regime, 1958–65), 193 (Burma under Ne Win, 1961), 248 (Senegal, 1961), 313 (Dahomey, 1963), 403 (Upper Volta, 1965), 419 (Congo Brazzaville, 1965), 448 (Uganda, 1965), 451 (Bolivia, 1965). Argentina under Perón was convicted on the same grounds (Case 12, 1950), as was Batista's Cuba (Case 159, 1956). The military regime in Brazil was convicted for putting all unions under its control (Case 385, 1965), as was the Ba'ath regime of Syria (Case 393, 1965).

16. Cases 239 (1960), 379 (1965), 444 (1965).

17. Case 125 (1955). Case 335 (Peru, 1965) illustrates a similar problem facing a struggling democratic regime.

18. Case 179 (1958–67).

19. Cases 134, 153 (1956).

20. Case 354 (1965).

21. Case 49 (1951). The defendant was the elected Muslim League government.

22. Case 415 (1965), St. Vincent.

23. Cases 140, 190, 192, 216 (1956–62, against the Frondizi and Illía governments) and Cases 273, 503 (1963, 1967, against military regimes).

24. Case 169 (1957).

25. Case 167 (1957).

26. Case 2 (1950) and Cases 72, 122 (1952–54).

27. Cases 348 (1964), 408 (1965), 423 (1965), 454 (1965). Ecuador, a traditional oligarchy, was convicted twice on very similar grounds (Cases 364 [1964] and 422 [1965]), though attempts to organize peasant unions were then involved. Convictions with almost identical content were also pronounced against Guatemala, at the time under authoritarian rule; but because the complaints were made in the backwash of the counterrevolution under Castillo Armas (and his successors), they were coded as being in the Cold War context (Cases 109 [1954], 131 [1955–56], 144 [1956]). Guatemala came close to being convicted once more before the installation

of the democratic Méndez Montenegro government for allegedly interfering with elections and recognition of the rubber workers union (Case 352 [1964–65]).

CHAPTER FIVE

1. For a full elaboration of these doctrines in their early forms, see Jenks, *Protection of Trade Union Freedom*. Jenks's most recent summary and evaluation of the human rights protection machinery he was so instrumental in establishing and nurturing is his "The International Protection of Trade Union Rights," in Evan Luard, ed., *The International Protection of Human Rights* (London: Thames and Hudson, 1967). His discussion of the fine line between trade union and political issues is most revealing. See pp. 222–23.

2. Cases 16 (France-Morocco, 1951–55), 17 and 61 (France-Tunisia, 1952, 1953), 156 (France-Algeria, 1956–62).

3. Cases 29 (U.K.–Kenya, 1951), 30 (U.K.–Malaya, 1952), and 24, 38, and 59 (U.K.–Cyprus, 1951, 1953).

4. The break in the Greek situation came with Case 185 (1958).

5. For South Africa, cf. Case 63 with Case 102 (1954), the first break in the earlier doctrine.

6. Cases 370 and 432 (1965). The committee was reluctant to entertain similar complaints against Spain until after she had rejoined the ILO. Cf. Case 53 (1952) with Case 143 (1956–62).

7. See, for instance, Cases 235 (Cameroun, 1960), 339 (Morocco, 1965), 363 (Colombia, 1964), 373 (Haiti, 1965), 381 (Honduras, 1965), and 418 (Cameroun, 1965).

8. Case 233 (Congo-Brazzaville, 1960–61). See 51st Report of the committee, *Official Bulletin*, XLIV (1961), 3, 220–23.

9. Case 419 (Congo-Brazzaville, 1965).

10. See, for instance, Cases 401 (Burundi, 1964–68), 364 and 422 (Ecuador, 1964, 1965), and 360 and 467 (Dominican Republic, 1965, 1966).

11. Case 420 (India, 1965–67). This complex case, which pits the Calcutta Port Commissioners Workers Union against the government of India, grew out of a series of allegations to the effect that the Port Commissioners were profiteering at the expense of workers in public housing under the Port Authority's jurisdiction, and that there was anti-union discrimination in disciplinary measures taken to eject squatters from the premises.

12. The cases of Greece, Japan, and Spain will be examined again in Chapter 6. Costa Rica and Libya were both "visited" by representatives (independent experts) of the ILO Director-General. The government of Burundi sent a special mission to Geneva to explain itself, "in the course

of which," says Jenks, "important assurances were given" (in Luard, *International Protection*, p. 227). Prior to the mission's appearance, the ILO had referred the Burundi case to the UN Commission on Human Rights.

13. 29th Report of the committee, *Official Bulletin*, XLIII (1960), 3, para. 6. See Jenks (*ibid.*, pp. 239f) for a much more unqualified and positive view of the impartiality and legitimacy of the committee. Though I would agree with the accuracy of Jenks's assessment during the most recent period, I must seriously disagree with its application to the period before 1957 or so.

14. For greater detail on the work of the UN General Assembly with respect to violations of human rights, see Evan Luard, "Promotion of Human Rights by UN Political Bodies"; and R. B. Ballinger, "UN Action on Human Rights in South Africa." in Luard, *International Protection*, pp. 132–49, 248–85.

CHAPTER SIX

1. Jenks, in Luard, *International Protection*, pp. 227–28.

2. *Ibid.*, pp. 244–45.

3. Cases 16 (France-Morocco, 1951–55), 136 (U.K.–Cyprus, 1955–59), 152 (U.K.–Northern Rhodesia, 1956–59), 421 (U.K.–Aden, 1965–67). Note, however, that even in these situations the compliance pattern is far from uniform. France failed to respond in Cases 75 (Madagascar, 1953) and 156 (Algeria, 1956–62); Britain was equally uncooperative in Cases 194 (Singapore, 1959–65), 291 (Aden, 1962–67) before the decision to withdraw had been made, and 366 (British Guiana, 1964), when it was the policy of the government to prevent the consolidation of power by Chedi Jagan and his affiliated unions.

4. Case 264 (1964).

5. Case 285 (1963).

6. Case 211 (1959–64).

7. Case 132 (1955).

8. Cases 179 (Japan, 1958–64), 125 (Brazil, 1955–58), and 134 and 154 (Chile, 1956).

9. Case 191 (1958–64).

10. Cases 172 and 258 (Argentina, 1958–60, 1961), 307 (Somalia, 1963–64), 341 (Greece, 1964–65), 221 (U.K.–Aden, 1960–62).

11. Cases 10 (Chile, 1951–52), 11 (Brazil, 1951), 48 (Japan, 1952), 121 (Greece, 1955).

12. Cases 251 and 298 (Southern Rhodesia, 1961–68, 1963–65), 415 (St. Vincent, 1965–66).

13. Cases 234 (Greece, 1961–62), 239 (Costa Rica, 1960–63), 335 (Peru, 1965–67), 354 (Chile, 1965), and 140 and 190 (Argentina, 1956, 1958–59).

14. Cases 506 (Liberia, 1967), 169 (Turkey, 1957), and 408 and 454 (Honduras, 1965, 1965–67).

15. Case 422 (1965–68).

16. Case 202 (1959–68).

17. Case 303 (1963–67).

18. Case 385 (1965–68).

19. Case 234 (1961–62).

20. Case 413 (1965). This account is based for the most part on the report of the Fact-Finding and Conciliation Commission, in *Official Bulletin* (Special Supplement), XLIX, 3 (July 1966). See also Jenks, in Luard, *International Protection*, pp. 234–35.

21. The Fact-Finding and Conciliation Commission's Solomonic judgment relies heavily on the doctrine of public interest in its finding that the request of one of the parties constitutes insufficient grounds for terminating the procedure. The panel held that it was charged with a public inquiry into general principles and their application in its fact-finding phase, rather than with giving satisfaction to the parties involved. This, obviously, was not true of the conciliation phase. Furthermore, the panel held that before consenting to a withdrawal it must satisfy itself the request is based on the freely expressed will of the parties, to be determined by hearing their opinion.

22. Case 519 (1967–).

23. My account rests almost entirely on Ehud Harari, "The Politics of Labor Legislation in Japan" (Ph.D. dissertation, University of California, Berkeley, 1968). This dissertation, based on field work in Japan and on extensive familiarity with Japanese sources and informants, is a comprehensive, thoughtful, and careful study. I wish to take this opportunity to express my deep gratitude to Professor Harari for reading and correcting my account of this episode, though whatever mistakes remain are mine alone.

24. Case 48 (1952). Case 60 (1953) was dismissed for lack of evidence.

CHAPTER SEVEN

1. As early as 1947 the "father of functionalism," David Mitrany, expressed misgivings about the relevance of the field of human rights for progressive value sharing ("Human Rights and International Organization," *India Quarterly*, III [1947], 115ff). He argued that the field was much too impregnated with *a priori*, conflict-laden aspirations to lend itself to the kind of evolution described in my study. He may yet turn out to be right. Note, however, this statement in *Proceedings of the American Society of International Law* (Washington, D.C., 1965), p. 139:

"The Chairman, Professor Urban G. Whitaker, in his opening remarks noted that attendance at the panel was sparse. This, Professor Whitaker felt, was unfortunate because the Specialized Agencies are developing international law faster than other, more political, organs of the United Nations system. It is in the technical, less spectacular world of the Specialized Agencies that international law is expanding new frontiers rapidly."

2. For evidence of widely divergent trends in the evolution of conceptions of basic human rights in Asia, see the articles by Romila Thapar and George Thambyahpillai, in "Human Rights in Perspective," *International Social Science Journal*, XVIII (1966), 1. In the same issue, however, Maria Hirszowicz suggests that Marxist conceptions of human rights, especially economic rights, are acquiring universal acceptance. William J. Goode, in his article "Family Patterns and Human Rights" (*ibid.*), also suggests an increasing universalization with respect to the rights of women and children in their domestic and occupational roles. Maurice Cranston, in *What Are Human Rights?* (New York: Basic Books, 1963), claims a uniquely Western base for human rights, insisting that economic and social aspirations cannot be logically assimilated into the Western emphasis on political rights for individuals, a claim disputed by D. D. Raphael in "The Liberal Western Tradition of Human Rights," *International Social Science Journal*, XVIII (1966), 1, 22–30.

3. Goode, p. 44.

4. The following documents suggest not only that the principles in question have received a very mixed reception but also that their proponents seem partly motivated by rhetorical considerations: "Draft Declaration on Social Development; Note by the Secretary-General," UN doc. A/7161, and "Draft Declaration on Social Development; Comments Received from Member States," UN doc. A/7235, 27 September 1968.

5. For an up-to-date description of the European Convention and its machinery, see A. H. Robertson, "The European Convention on Human Rights," in Luard, *International Protection*, pp. 99–131. On the Inter-American Commission, see L. Ronald Scheman, "The Inter-American Commission on Human Rights," *American Journal of International Law*, 1965, p. 335; Cabranes, "The Protection of Human Rights by the Organization of American States," *ibid.*, 1968, p. 888.

6. Stanley Hoffmann, in Lawrence Scheinman and David Wilkinson, eds., *International Law and Political Crisis* (Boston: Little, Brown, 1968), p. xvii. A survey conducted by UNITAR disclosed that one reason governments commonly give for not ratifying human rights conventions is that in so doing they become subject, in particular, to the substantive content of the treaty! UNITAR, "Acceptance of Human Rights Conventions," UN doc. A/CONF. 32/15, 28 March 1968, p. 11. In the U.S. most of the peace-through-law movement and activities of the Anti-Defamation League illus-

trate the "law first" approach. For a lucid and succinct example, see Egon Schwelb, *Human Rights and the International Community* (Chicago: Quadrangle Books, 1964).

7. See, for example, William D. Coplin, "International Law and Assumptions about the State System," in R. Falk and W. Hanrieder, eds., *International Law and Organization* (New York: Lippincott, 1968), pp. 15–34. See also Gerhard Niemeyer, *Law Without Force* (Princeton, N.J.: Princeton University Press, 1941).

8. The League system has been studied extensively. See C. A. Macartney, "League of Nations' Protection of Minority Rights," in Luard, *International Protection*, pp. 22–38. See also Inis L. Claude, Jr., *National Minorities: An International Problem* (Cambridge, Mass.: Harvard University Press, 1955). Moses Moskowitz, *Human Rights and World Order* (New York: Oceana, 1958), pp. 117–30, traces the evolution of the right of individual petition to the League in the context of minority treaties, a development not foreseen in 1919 by the drafters of the treaties. The experiment of international protection of minority rights through standing machinery and individual petition lasted longest in the case of Upper Silesia. In addition to Ganji, *International Protection*, see Georges Kaeckenbeeck, *The International Experiment of Upper Silesia* (London: Oxford University Press, 1942).

Nor should it be forgotten that the Trusteeship System facilitated the evolution of the right of individual petition, both written and oral, to UN bodies. In the course of reviewing the record of nations administering trust territories, UN organs were often called on to examine allegations of violations of rights spelled out in the Universal Declaration of Human Rights. At the same time, it should be recalled that though this supervisory activity could and did influence the policies of France, Britain, the U.S., Australia, and New Zealand, there was nothing the UN could do to preserve these rights once the trusts had been liquidated.

9. See Thomas Buergenthal, "The United Nations and the Development of Rules Relating to Human Rights," *Proceedings of the American Society of International Law* (Washington, D.C., 1965), pp. 132–36. Buergenthal ingeniously demonstrates that the UN Commission on Human Rights, contrary to its actual policy, could have interpreted Articles 55 and 56 of the Charter and the Universal Declaration of Human Rights *together* in such a way as to create a UN jurisdiction over violations of human rights involving discrimination, though not over generalized violations. This interpretation is strengthened further by the wording of the Declaration on the Elimination of All Forms of Racial Discrimination, General Assembly res. 1904 (XVIII), November 20, 1963. Furthermore, such an interpretation could have given the commission the power to investigate specific allegations of violations, powers claimed and exercised by the Assembly's Special Committee on Colonialism, for instance.

10. For an elaboration of this systemic projection, see Ernst B. Haas, *Collective Security and the Future International System* (Denver: University of Denver Monograph Series in World Affairs, 1968), and R. Falk and C. Black, eds., *The Future of the International Legal Order*, Vol. I (Princeton, N.J.: Princeton University Press, 1969); a shortened version is included in Falk and Hanrieder.

11. On this topic, see Sir Samuel Hoare, "The UN Commission on Human Rights," in Luard, *International Protection*, pp. 59–98. This is the most up-to-date and objective summary of the commission's work I have discovered. See also Rosalyn Higgins, "Technical Assistance for Human Rights: A New Approach to an Old Problem," *The World Today* (April and May 1963). Apparently René Cassin also shared this view, since he praised the advisory services program as a necessary prerequisite for eventual UN convention-drafting. See Albert Verdoot, *Naissance et Signification de la Déclaration Universelle des Droits de l'Homme* (Louvain and Paris: Editions Nauwdaerts, 1964), pp. 325–28.

12. William Korey, "The Key to Human Rights—Implementation," *International Conciliation*, No. 570 (November 1968), p. 62.

13. For evidence, see Haas, *Beyond the Nation-State*, pp. 250–69, 310–26, 370–80.

14. Before the current inquiry against Greece, only two such cases had ever arisen, both involving charges of forced labor. In the first, Ghana registered a complaint against Portuguese policy in Africa and obtained some satisfaction; in the second, Portugal lodged a complaint against Liberia and got much less satisfaction. For details, see *ibid.*, pp. 361–70.

15. See Pieter N. Drost, *Human Rights as Legal Rights* (Leiden: Sijthoff, 1965), especially Chapter 18. Grenville Clark and Louis B. Sohn make their proposals for an amended UN Charter with a Bill of Rights entirely on a positivist basis by stressing treaties, thus suggesting that a positive law of human rights is yet to be created. *World Peace Through World Law* (Cambridge, Mass.: Harvard University Press, 1958), pp. 350–51.

16. J. L. Brierly, *The Law of Nations*, 5th ed. (Oxford: Clarendon Press, 1955), p. 60. My emphasis.

17. I am paraphrasing the argument of Amitai Etzioni, who speaks here for much of the activist intellectual community seeking to combine objective knowledge with social commitment and action. *The Active Society* (New York: Free Press, 1968), especially pp. 575–76, 602–8.

18. *Ibid.*, p. 608.

19. Advisory Opinion, Reservations on the Convention on the Prevention and Punishment of Genocide, ICJ, *Reports*, 1951, p. 23. My emphasis. This opinion is cited by Taubenfeld and Taubenfeld (pp. 62–63) as part of their general argument to show the role of non-consensual forces in the growth of a customary international law favoring universal human rights. Their argument, however, is weakened considerably because various learned

judges on the court, in hinting that some principles of natural law exist despite their non-recognition in positive law, have invariably cited texts such as the UN Charter, the ILO Constitution, and human rights conventions; in short, they took refuge in that safe haven of positivism: treaties.

20. For a trenchant analysis of the ICJ's decision in the Southwest Africa cases, see Richard A. Falk, "The South West Africa Cases: An Appraisal," *International Organization*, XXI, 1 (Winter 1967), 1–22.

21. Oscar Schachter, "The Relations of Law, Politics and Actions in the United Nations," *Recueil des Cours*, II (1963); cited by Taubenfeld and Taubenfeld, p. 63. Emphasis supplied by the Taubenfelds. For an explicit claim that the protection of private groups by international law must be based on the natural law doctrine, see J. J. Lador-Lederer, *International Group Protection: Aims and Methods of Human Rights* (Leiden: Sijthoff, 1968), pp. 9–12. This work contains a great deal of legal and historical material on attempts by international organizations and tribunals to protect group rights. The author seeks to show that the evolution of positive law increasingly approximates the ethical standards of natural law. Unfortunately, almost no data are advanced with respect to the implementation of this law. Moreover, the typology of regimes used is too primitive to permit a strong ordering of the legal data.

22. I have relied on Myres S. McDougal, H. D. Lasswell, and J. L. Miller, *The Interpretation of Agreements and World Public Order* (New Haven, Conn.: Yale University Press, 1967); and Myres S. McDougal, Harold D. Lasswell, and W. Michael Reisman, "Theories about International Law: Prologue to a Configurative Jurisprudence," *Virginia Journal of International Law*, VIII, 2 (April 1968). I wish to thank Professor Harold Lasswell for permitting me to see parts of an unpublished MS further elaborating these ideas. See also the incisive commentaries of Richard A. Falk, in *Virginia Journal of International Law*, I, 2 (April 1968), and Gidon Gottlieb, in *World Politics*, October 1968.

23. McDougal, Lasswell, and Miller, p. 44. I confess to some uncertainty in interpreting—configuratively, functionally, or otherwise—the concept of public order. At times I have a feeling reference is made to whatever vestiges of public order inhere in the current decentralized and diffuse international legal system; at other times the reference seems to be a desired future state of affairs. Since the overriding norm of human dignity informs the process of treaty interpretation, it is of some importance to know whether that norm is available here and now, or whether it is merely immanent in world social evolution. Finally, since the ideal of human dignity is also defined in terms of "free political action under law," it is not clear to me what happens when dignity and public order come into conflict.

24. This point is forcefully made by Falk, in *Virginia Journal of International Law*, pp. 352–54. Falk stresses instead the "existential loneliness"

of the treaty interpreter, who should be conscious of all the deliberate misunderstandings that divide the parties and all the gaps in the law that make difficult a solution advancing an international legal order, without deceiving himself about the contribution he alone can make. But Falk, in singling out for special study those polito-legal conflicts that are uppermost in his mind with respect to norms that require assertion, substitutes a natural law formula of his own when he encourages the interpreter to act on his own private normative preferences and support them with whatever evidences of more general consensus he can discover.

METHODOLOGICAL APPENDIX

1. R. W. Cox and H. K. Jacobson, "Decision-Making in International Organizations: An Interim Report" (paper delivered at the 65th Annual Meeting of the American Political Science Association, New York, September 1969). (Mimeo.)

2. For further details on this approach, see Ernst B. Haas, *Tangle of Hopes* (Englewood Cliffs, N.J.: Prentice-Hall, 1969), Chapter 2.

3. Cox and Jacobson, pp. 48–49.

Index